THE APPLIQUÉ BOOK

Traditional Techniques, Modern Style
16 QUILT PROJECTS

Casey York

stash BOOKS.
an imprint of C&T Publishing

Text copyright © 2016 by Casey York

Photography and artwork copyright © 2016 by C&T Publishing, Inc.

PUBLISHER: Amy Marson

CREATIVE DIRECTOR: Gailen Runge

EDITOR: Karla Menaugh

TECHNICAL EDITORS: Alison M. Schmidt and Gailen Runge

COVER/BOOK DESIGNER: April Mostek

PRODUCTION COORDINATOR / ILLUSTRATOR: Freesia Pearson Blizard

PRODUCTION EDITORS: Joanna Burgarino and Jessie Brotman

PHOTO ASSISTANT: Sarah Frost

STYLE PHOTOGRAPHY by Nissa Brehmer and
INSTRUCTIONAL PHOTOGRAPHY by Diane Pedersen,
unless otherwise noted

Published by Stash Books, an imprint of C&T Publishing, Inc., P.O. Box 1456, Lafayette, CA 94549

Library of Congress Cataloging-in-Publication Data

York, Casey, 1979- author.

The appliqué book : traditional techniques, modern style--16 quilt projects / Casey York.

   pages cm

ISBN 978-1-61745-121-8 (soft cover)

1. Quilts. 2. Quilting. 3. Appliqué--Patterns. I. Title.

TT835.Y658 2016

746.46--dc23

                    2015027786

Printed in China

10 9 8 7 6 5 4 3 2 1

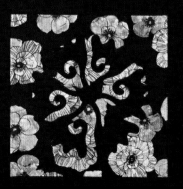

Dedication

This book is dedicated to the Modern Quilt Guild and its members, as well as to any self-identified "modern" quilters who aren't afraid of trying something new.

Acknowledgments

Any book owes its existence to many people besides the author. For a compilation book like this one, the list grows even longer. I regret that I cannot list every person who participated in this book by name, but please rest assured that you have my genuine gratitude.

This book would not exist without its contributing authors. From their interest and eagerness in participating in this project to their beautiful projects and clear instructions, they truly went above and beyond to make this a delightful book that I hope you will enjoy. I also owe enormous thanks to the subjects of the profiles that you will find throughout the book; I hope that through them you will come to appreciate the vast possibilities that appliqué offers modern quilters.

Creating a compilation has been a new type of project for me, and I owe many thanks to my developmental editor, Karla Menaugh, for guiding me through the process. I feel so lucky to have been able to work with a technical editor, and in this book it has been my pleasure to collaborate with Alison Schmidt. My production editors, Joanna Burgarino and Jessie Brotman, and production coordinator, Freesia Pearson Blizard, took things from there and ensured that this book progressed smoothly from manuscript to finished product. I owe the gorgeous design to April Mostek, who ensured that seeing the initial pages for the first time was a thrilling experience. As always, it has been my pleasure to work with Lynn Merill, Jocelyn Portacio, and the rest of the publicity team at C&T. Finally, many thanks to Roxane Cerda for patiently and enthusiastically putting up with my endless questions.

My husband, Barrett, has been instrumental in guiding this, my first venture into managing a group project; I couldn't have done it without his insights and support. My sons, Julian and Simon, were bright rays of encouragement as they watched me work on each aspect of this book, and I am just as grateful for their patience with me. My extended family has been wonderfully supportive, and I feel so lucky to have had them behind me in the venture. And I will continually be grateful for the friendship and support of the St. Louis Modern Quilt Guild, as well as the many, many people I have been so fortunate to meet in this industry. You know who you are—sincerely, thank you.

Contents

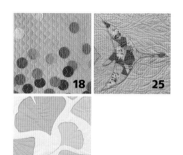

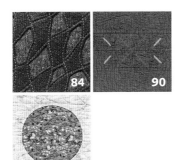

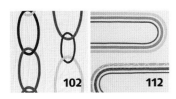

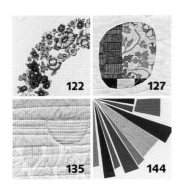

Foreword by Cindy Lammon

Modern appliqué—I am beyond excited to see these two words together!

My interest in appliqué began in the early 1990s, when Baltimore Album appliqué quilts were experiencing a renaissance fueled by amazing designers like Elly Sienkiewicz. When a group of quilters in my local guild decided to start a Baltimore Album quilt, I jumped in with both feet. The quilt took me a couple of years to complete, but I learned to love the process. And that first appliqué quilt was juried into the American Quilter's Society Show and the Quilter's Heritage Show in 1994. It taught me an important lesson that has fueled much of my quilting career: never be afraid to try something new.

I met Casey York at the St. Louis Modern Quilt Guild. I was amazed by how fearlessly she took on projects, often asking questions about technique but always maintaining her unique modern design aesthetic. Casey's first book, *Modern Appliqué Illusions*, showcases not only her modern design skills but techniques perfectly suited for today's modern appliqué designs.

One thing I know for sure is that trying something new is the best way to keep your interest and excitement alive. Appliqué techniques are quite varied, so be sure to try several or even all of them. I think you'll find that there is a comfortable technique for every quilter and every project!

This book showcases both established and new ways to create innovative designs that embody the characteristics of modern quilting. The contributors are definitely forward thinkers, and I'm very excited to witness the journey that appliqué is taking in the modern quilting movement!

....

Photo by Cheryl Alsup-Brown

CINDY LAMMON began sewing as a small child at her mother's and grandmother's side. She took a beginner quilting class in 1981 and started what would become a lifelong passion. Cindy has authored four books, all combining her love of piecing and appliqué: *Gathered From the Garden, Flower Pots, Flowers All Around*, and *Simply Modern Christmas*.

INTRODUCTION

Appliqué is one of the oldest textile arts. Spanning multiple continents and cultures, the process of appliqué is simply that of "applying" one fabric on top of another to make a scene or decorative arrangement. It is one of the simplest concepts in quiltmaking, and yet also one of the richest and most varied.

Appliqué offers the modern quilter a new world of design possibilities. Because appliqués can be cut into any imaginable shape and can be placed anywhere on the background, appliqué techniques offer a creative freedom that the geometry of piecing prohibits. Not only naturalistic but also abstract and improvisational elements can be cut—sometimes freehand—from fabric and arranged anywhere on the surface of the quilt without resorting to complicated quilt math. And these elements can be applied to all types of items, not just quilts. Indeed, appliqué is one of the easiest and most popular ways to embellish clothing, pillows, and home decor items.

Appliqué is an ideal family of techniques for those who adhere to the Slow Sewing movement, which encourages us to slow down and be mindful of the process of creating. And it is an inviting and forgiving method of quiltmaking that I believe you will find by turns relaxing and exhilarating.

This book showcases project ideas from leading modern designers who make wonderful appliqué quilts and other textiles using a variety of methods. Some of these methods are complex, while others are simple. Some are time-consuming, while others are quick to complete. Some are precise and structured, while others are free-form and improvisational.

One of the beauties of appliqué is that you can mix and match patterns and techniques. The quilters' projects are grouped by basic technique, with information on each technique presented in a special chapter at the beginning of each section. You can choose to make the projects using the quilters' original construction methods or a different technique.

I hope that reading and using this book inspires you to try appliqué, whether you choose one or many techniques.

Once you become comfortable with a technique or two, try designing your own appliqués. All you need is a shape you can trace, an idea for how to use it in a quilt or other project, and beautiful fabric to make your design idea a reality. Becoming comfortable with appliqué will open many new design avenues for you and provide you with an enjoyable process for creating spectacular products.

Materials

Appliqué techniques are diverse and call for diverse supplies. Invest in the best quality that you can afford. Using high-quality materials and supplies will increase your probability of success and your enjoyment of the process. See Resources (page 157) for information about where to buy materials.

Pattern

The patterns used for the projects in this book are on the double-sided pullout page in the back. Unless otherwise noted, all have been reversed for transferring onto the wrong side of your appliqué fabrics. Some techniques, such as needle-turn appliqué, use patterns in the same orientation as the finished project. When this is the case, it is noted on the pattern.

Don't feel limited to using these patterns, though! If you can draw or trace a shape from another image, you can turn it into an appliqué.

Fabric

I prefer to use all natural fibers, although some synthetic fibers can yield great results. I encourage you to experiment.

Quilters favor 100% cotton fabric because it has an even weave, is easy to stitch, and comes in myriad colors and prints.

Other natural fibers, such as silk and wool, also can be used to great effect in appliqué. However, because they can shrink and fray in different ways, you should prewash these fibers if you plan to wash the finished project.

Be careful when using synthetic fibers because they are more susceptible to heat.

TIP Most quilting cotton is 45″ wide. However, it is generally safer to assume a width of 40″ due to differences in the width of selvages and possible printing and cutting imperfections. All the project yardages given in this book assume a usable width of 40″.

MATERIALS ⟶

A: Fusible web

B: Wash-away appliqué paper

C: Freezer paper

D: Glues

E: Glue applicators

F: Starch, brush, bowl

G: Silicone Release Paper (by C&T Publishing)

H: Appliqué pressing sheet

I: Template plastic

J: Rotary cutter

K: Paper scissors

L: Embroidery scissors

M: Fabric scissors used with paper-backed fusible web

N: Fabric scissors used only for fabric

O: Alex Anderson 4-in-1 Essential Sewing Tool with seam ripper and tips for turning and fingerpressing (by C&T Publishing)

P: Marking tools

Q: Cotton thread for bobbin for appliqué

R: Invisible thread for appliqué

S: Hoop for embroidery

T: Embroidery floss

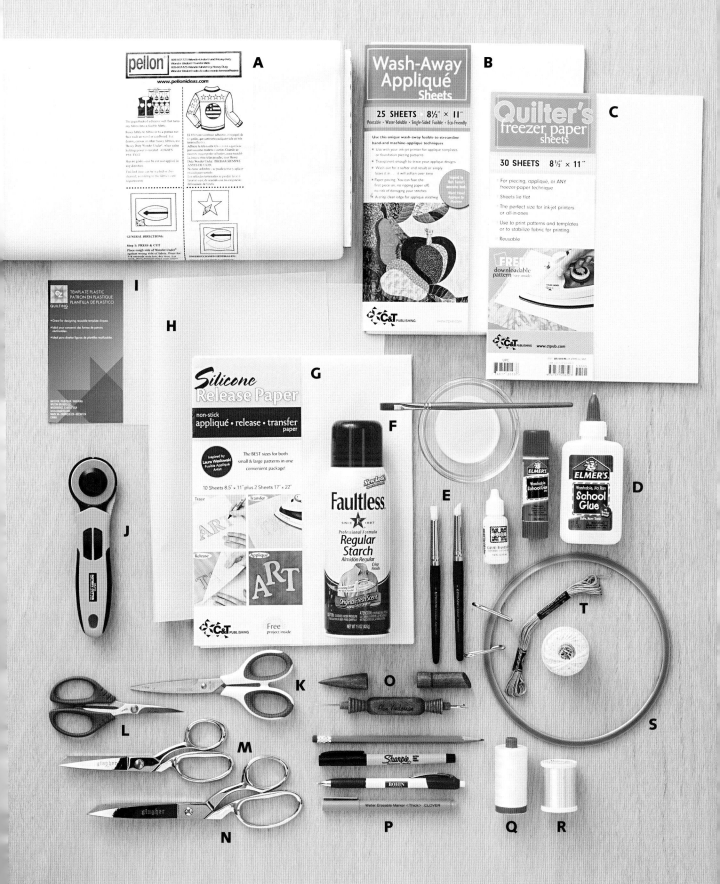

Thread

Thread is labeled according to the diameter of the strand, known as the thread's "weight." The higher the number, the finer the thread. Because appliqué stitches often are visible on the top of the quilt, the weight and color of the thread contribute to the finished design.

Whether stitching by machine or by hand, I prefer to use a 40- or 50-weight 100% cotton thread in a color that matches the appliqué fabric. I recommend that you experiment with different weights and colors to find the combination that appeals to you.

If you don't want your appliqué stitches to show, try invisible thread. My favorite is Superior Clear MonoPoly, a polyester thread that behaves like a cotton thread in the machine but gives an invisible stitch. Aurifil also makes an invisible nylon thread that gives very good results in a variety of machines. Invisible thread can sometimes be difficult to wind on a bobbin, so I like to pair it with 50-weight cotton thread in the bobbin, in a color that matches the background fabric.

Fusible Web

Fusible web is a heat-activated adhesive that allows you to use an iron to bond fabrics together. Many varieties have paper backings, which make it easy to transfer your appliqué patterns directly onto the wrong side of the appliqué fabrics. After you cut out the appliqués, you can fuse them to the background fabric in preparation for stitching. Fusible web's glue-like texture helps reduce, but does not eliminate, fraying in raw-edge appliqué.

Buy the lightest weight of web available from your chosen brand. Heavier weights can add stiffness and bulk to your quilts. My favorite is regular-weight 805 Wonder-Under (by Pellon). This product includes a single paper backing, making tracing templates straightforward, and it fuses quickly and easily to fabrics without adding stiffness. If your quilt is to be washed, you will need to stitch the appliqués to the background, and Wonder-Under can be sewn by machine and by hand.

Freezer Paper

Freezer paper has a shiny, waxy side that adheres to fabric when heated and peels away cleanly. You can find freezer paper at your grocery store in the food-wrap section, as well as at some craft stores. Some stores even stock printable freezer-paper sheets, such as Quilter's Freezer Paper Sheets (from C&T Publishing), which can be put through an inkjet printer.

NOTE: Never put printable freezer paper through a laser printer or photocopier, both of which use heat and will make a sticky mess of the paper.

Wash-Away Appliqué Paper

Fusible wash-away appliqué paper, available in 8½″ × 11″ sheets and on a wider roll, is an alternative to freezer paper. It can be fused to the wrong side of fabric for use in turned-edge techniques but will dissolve in water within one or two washings. If you use glue to secure your turned edges, using Wash-Away Appliqué Sheets or Wash-Away Appliqué Roll (both by C&T Publishing) allows you to avoid cutting into the back side of the quilt top to remove the templates after stitching.

Template Plastic

Translucent sheets of template plastic allow you to create reusable templates that will not shrink, curl, or wrinkle as paper would. You can cut out plastic templates using a craft knife or scissors. Templates are reversible, so be sure to label the right and wrong sides for easy reference. Some, but not all, template plastic is heat resistant and can be used with an iron. Follow the manufacturer's recommendations when it comes to applying heat.

Starch and Paintbrush

Spray starch and the heat from an iron provide an alternative to glue when turning under appliqué edges. Spray a good quantity of starch into a dish and use a paintbrush to apply it precisely to the edge seam allowances; then use the iron to press into place. For use with freezer paper, see Freezer Paper and Starch Technique (page 50).

Glues and Applicators

Washable glue can be incredibly useful for turning under appliqué edges and for basting appliqués to the background fabric. Many quiltmakers swear by using a regular washable glue stick to secure the turned edges of their appliqués. See Turned-Edge Appliqué (page 42).

Rubber-tipped color-shaper tools, such as Colour Applicators (by Pro Arte), make it easy to apply glue from a glue stick precisely without getting your fingers sticky.

You can use special appliqué glue or regular washable white school glue to secure appliqués to the background fabric for stitching. See Basting Appliqués (page 15). Only a very small amount of glue is necessary for basting, so a fine-tipped applicator bottle can be useful.

Scissors

The paper backings on fusible web and freezer paper can dull scissor blades, so I recommend using a separate pair of scissors dedicated to cutting paper.

If you find yourself cutting through both fabric and paper, as with the raw-edge appliqué technique, you may want to dedicate another pair of scissors to cutting fabric and paper together.

A pair of small embroidery scissors is invaluable for clipping small threads close to the surface of your fabric, as well as for cutting away the top layer of fabric in some types of reverse appliqué.

Die Cutting Machine

Although none of the projects in this book use a die cutter, it is a wonderful tool for raw-edge appliqué because it can cut fabric into intricate shapes quickly and accurately. You can cut fabric alone or create fusible appliqués by applying fusible web to your fabrics before putting them through the cutter. For needle-turn appliqué, you can use a die cutter to cut some simple geometric shapes, such as circles. More intricate shapes would lack the seam allowance necessary for turning under.

Rotary Cutter, Ruler, and Mat

A rotary cutter makes quick work of cutting fabric into shapes with straight edges. Many of the projects in this book feature rotary-cut elements, such as block backgrounds. Some even feature rotary-cut appliqués. See Shards (page 145).

Bias-Tape Maker

There are various ways to make the flexible fabric strips used in bias appliqué, but my favorite is to use a bias-tape maker. Simply cut strips of fabric on the bias in the width required by the size of tape maker you are using. Feed the strips through the simple folding mechanism and press with steam for perfect bias strips with no burned fingers.

Marking Tools

I recommend a fine-tipped permanent marker for tracing patterns onto materials like freezer paper and fusible web. Pencils work too but have a tendency to smear. If you need to mark the fabric itself, as in needle-turn appliqué, a very sharp pencil will work, but a removable fabric marker is even better. A white-leaded pencil can be useful to have on hand for marking dark fabrics. If your appliqué method involves heat, be sure to test how your removable fabric marker reacts to an iron.

Iron

A hot iron is essential for most of the techniques in this book. Often, steam can help you achieve crisply creased edges, but in some cases—such as when you are using fusibles—a dry iron is preferred.

A mini iron can be very useful for turning under the slender seam allowances of turned-edge appliqués. If you are using fusible web, it is also very useful to have some iron cleaner on hand, along with a couple of cleaning cloths.

Nonstick Appliqué Pressing Sheet

If you are using glue to secure turned edges, nonstick surfaces can be indispensable. Nonstick pressing sheets protect your iron and ironing surface from adhesive residue, and the appliqués peel right off once they cool. C&T Publishing's Silicone Release Paper also performs this function well.

Sewing Machine

Modern sewing machines offer many decorative stitches that you can use to stitch the edges of appliqués. However, all the projects in this book can be made with a machine with basic capabilities. Your machine should be capable of producing a zigzag stitch. A blanket stitch can be nice but is not necessary. Look for other useful features, such as the ability to control the length and width of the stitches, an automatic needle-down feature for pivoting, and a clear plastic open-toe presser foot so that you can see your stitches easily.

Needles

For machine stitching, I find that the sharp point of a fine microtex needle works best. I usually use a size 70/10 microtex needle.

For handwork, what matters most is how comfortable you are with the needle. Experiment with a variety of types and sizes to learn which ones suit you best. Consider the size of the eye and the size of the thread you will be using. The needle's diameter must make a hole in the fabric that is large enough for the thread to pass through without undue friction, which can cause the thread to fray. The size of the eye must also accommodate the bulk of the thread and should make it easy to thread the needle.

TIP The eyes of needles are punched through the metal, making the eye bigger and smoother on one side of the needle. If you are having trouble threading your needle, try turning it around to thread from the opposite side.

Turning Tool

For stitch-and-turn appliqué (page 50), you will need a turning tool to smooth out the edges of the appliqué. Alex Anderson's 4-in-1 Essential Sewing Tool is great because it contains several tools, but you also could use a chopstick.

Embroidery Supplies

If you choose to embellish your appliqué or finish its edges with embroidery, you will need special materials. First, invest in high-quality embroidery thread. I usually use three strands of six-stranded cotton embroidery floss. Many types of embroidery thread are available, so experiment to learn what works best for your projects.

You also may need an embroidery hoop to hold your fabric taut while you work the stitches. I favor spring-tension hoops, which make it easy to reposition my work and to adjust the tension as I am stitching.

Finally, invest in some dedicated embroidery needles. These have longer eyes than regular hand-sewing needles, making it easier to thread multiple strands of embroidery floss.

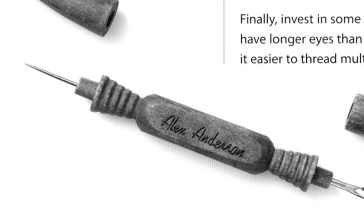

Basic Machine Appliqué

Unless you are doing needle-turn appliqué (page 43), you will probably be using a sewing machine to stitch down your appliqués. A number of different machine stitches can be used to secure appliqués to the background fabric, and the one you choose depends on how you want the finished project to look. The following stitches can be used on both raw-edge and turned-edge appliqués, but the basic principles remain the same. For more information on preparing appliqués, see Raw-Edge Appliqué (page 18) and Turned-Edge Appliqué (page 42).

Basting Appliqués

Unless you are using fusible web to adhere your appliqués to the background fabric, you will need to baste them in place prior to stitching. There are various ways to do this.

- You can use a running stitch to stitch the appliqués to the background. Use stitches that are ¼″ to ½″ long, placed ¼″ inside the outer edge of the appliqué (or ¼″ inside the traced stitching line if you are doing needle-turn appliqué).

- You can use appliqué glue or standard white school glue, both of which are water soluble and will wash out of your finished project. You need only a tiny dot of glue every couple of inches or so to hold your appliqué firmly to the background; it helps to dispense the glue from a narrow-tipped applicator bottle. Once the glue has dried, it will hold the appliqué securely in place for stitching.

- You can use appliqué pins to secure the appliqués to the background before they are stitched down.

Basic Machine-Appliqué Stitches

Straight Stitch

The straight stitch is an easy machine-appliqué stitch; you simply topstitch close to the edge of the appliqué to adhere the appliqué to the background fabric. In raw-edge appliqué, this stitch will *not* protect the edges of the appliqué fabric and will result in more fraying than if you used a stitch that extends over the edges of the appliqué.

For an interesting visual effect, try straight stitching around the appliqué multiple times to create a line of stitching that looks as if it were sketched.

Detail

Zigzag Stitch

The zigzag stitch can vary in width and length, depending on the effect you are seeking. A very short zigzag stitch will take on the appearance of satin stitching and protect the raw edges of the appliqué fabric better. A longer zigzag stitch will result in more fraying along the raw edges of the appliqué fabric, but not as much as if a straight stitch were used. A zigzag stitch can also be used with turned appliqué edges.

Detail

Detail

Blanket Stitch

The blanket stitch is also well suited to stitching around appliqués and will result in less fraying of raw-edge appliqué edges than will straight stitching.

Detail

TIP With both the blanket stitch and the zigzag stitch, the outside edge of the stitch should fall directly adjacent to the appliqué fabric, and the inner swing of the stitch should take a "bite" out of the appliqué fabric. The size of this bite will be determined by the width of the stitch. You can use very narrow stitches with turned-edge appliqué because of the seam allowance. However, with raw edges, the bite should be at least ⅛″ in order to ensure that the appliqués remain securely fastened to the background fabric even if the appliqué fabric frays a bit.

Stitching Techniques

Stitching around Curves and Corners

Go slowly when stitching around your appliqués to ensure that you accurately follow their edges. You will be able to go around gentle curves without stopping, but tighter curves and corners will require you to stop your machine with the needle down, raise the presser foot, and pivot the fabric. If you are using a blanket or zigzag stitch, make sure that you pivot when the needle is down on the outer swing of the stitch—when it is in the background fabric adjacent to the appliqué.

Ending the Line of Stitching

If you are using invisible thread, the easiest way to end your stitching when you have stitched all the way around an appliqué is to overlap a few stitches to lock them in place. Because the thread is invisible, the overlapping stitches will not show.

If you are using cotton thread, overlapping your stitches will show. Instead, leave long thread tails both when you start stitching and when you finish. Pull these to the back of the piece and tie them off.

RAW-EDGE APPLIQUÉ

In raw-edge appliqué, each fabric shape is cut along the edge of the pattern. There is no seam allowance, so no need to turn under the appliqué edges.

This family of techniques is ideal when shapes are too small or intricate for turned edges. It's also perfect for those of us who prefer instant gratification. With raw-edge appliqué, you can go immediately from transferring and cutting out appliqués to sewing them to the background.

The use of fusible web, while not essential, makes the process even faster by eliminating the need to baste the appliqués to the background.

The primary disadvantage of raw-edge appliqué is that, left exposed, raw fabric edges will begin to fray with time and use. In many instances this fraying adds texture and interest to the finished project, becoming a positive feature instead of a drawback. If, however, you do not like the look of slightly frayed appliqué edges, you have several options.

One is to use a dense machine zigzag or satin stitch to completely cover the appliqué edges. Another, featured in *Ginkgo Bed Runner* (page 36) and *Migrations Quilt Sampler* (page 29), is to encase raw edges beneath a line of machine or hand embroidery. Each method has its own distinctive look, will protect the edges from fraying, and will maintain the appearance of a smooth outline by drawing attention to the stitching line.

Basic Techniques

Raw-edge appliqué is fairly straightforward, and a wide variety of techniques are available to the quilter who wants to try this method. The following is a brief list of some of the most popular techniques.

Fusible Raw-Edge Appliqué

Fusible web—a thin layer of heat-activated adhesive that often has a paper backing on one or both sides—provides a way to both transfer your appliqué pattern to your fabric and then attach the resulting fabric appliqué to the background fabric.

If you are using your own appliqué patterns, be sure to reverse them before tracing onto the web. The shape you trace should be the mirror image of how you want the final appliqué to look.

TIP The appliqué patterns for projects in this book that use fusible appliqué or another method that transfers the pattern to the *wrong* side of the appliqué fabric have already been reversed. For the projects that use needle-turn appliqué or adhere the pattern to the *right* side of the fabric, the patterns do not need to be reversed. If you choose a different method for appliqué than the one used in the project, test the pattern to make sure it will be oriented the way you would like it when finished.

1 If you are using fusible web with a single paper backing, distinguish between the smooth side (the paper) and the slightly rough side (the fusible adhesive). Place the web with the rough side down on top of the appliqué pattern and trace the lines onto the paper backing.

If you are using web with 2 paper backings, consult the manufacturer's directions to determine the side onto which you should trace.

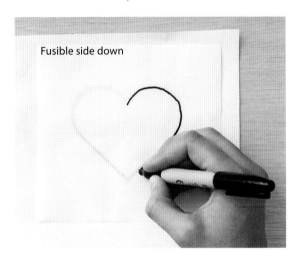

Fusible side down

2 Cut out the appliqué pattern, leaving about ¼″ outside the traced lines.

To prevent the fusible web from adding too much stiffness to large appliqués, it can be helpful to "window" it. To do this, simply cut away the fusible ¼˝ to ½˝ inside the traced lines as well, leaving a fusible "outline."

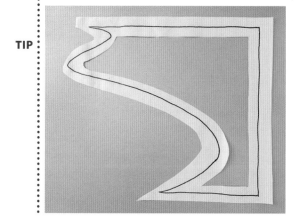

Each brand of fusible web requires slightly different heat settings and lengths of pressing time. Always follow the manufacturer's instructions.

4 Cut the fabric along the lines you traced onto the paper backing of the web. The extra paper around the edge of the traced lines will give your fabric a little extra stiffness and body, making it easier to cut along the lines accurately.

3 Place the appliqué fabric wrong side up on an ironing surface, and place the appliqué template on top of the fabric with the rough side facing down. In most cases, you will be able to see through the fusible and its paper backing so that you can position it precisely over the pattern in your fabric; this makes fusible web ideal if you want to fussy-cut motifs for your appliqué. Follow the manufacturer's directions to fuse the template to the fabric.

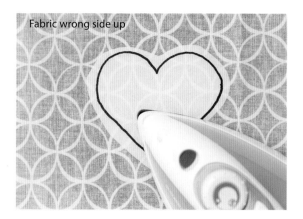
Fabric wrong side up

5 Peel the paper backing away from the fabric, making sure that the adhesive is sticking to the fabric instead of the paper.

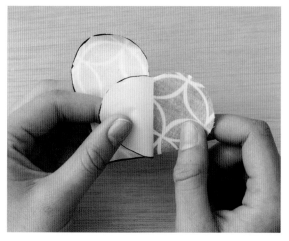

6 Position the appliqué on the right side of the background fabric with the adhesive facing down and the right side of the appliqué fabric facing up. Pin in place so that it doesn't shift when you move it to your pressing surface.

> **TIP** Minimal pinning is necessary with fusible web appliqué. I usually use one or two pins to anchor my pieces in place so they don't shift position when I move the background fabric to the ironing board. If the pieces move during this process, you can easily reposition them after you have smoothed out the background fabric on the ironing surface.

7 Using a nonstick appliqué pressing sheet between your iron and the appliqué, and following the manufacturer's directions, press the appliqué to adhere it permanently to the background fabric.

8 Stitch around the appliqué using your choice of stitches. See Basic Machine-Appliqué Stitches (page 16).

Nonfusible Raw-Edge Appliqué

This nonfusible raw-edge appliqué method uses freezer paper to easily transfer patterns to the fabric and give it some stiffness, which aids in accurately cutting out the appliqués.

1 Place a sheet of freezer paper with the shiny side down over the pattern. Use a pencil or fine-tipped permanent marker to trace the pattern onto the dull side of the freezer paper.

Shiny side down

2 Cut out the freezer-paper template roughly, leaving approximately ¼″ outside the traced lines.

3 Place the appliqué fabric on a pressing surface with the wrong side facing up. Place the freezer-paper template on top with the shiny side against the fabric. Use an iron to adhere the paper temporarily to the fabric.

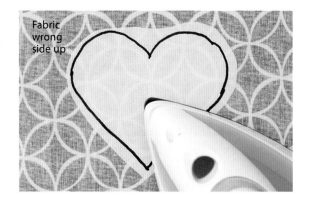

Fabric wrong side up

TIP If the appliqué method you would like to use differs from the project instructions, refer to Tip (page 19).

4 Cut out the appliqué along the traced lines. Then peel away the freezer paper, leaving just the fabric appliqué.

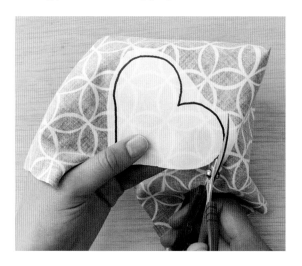 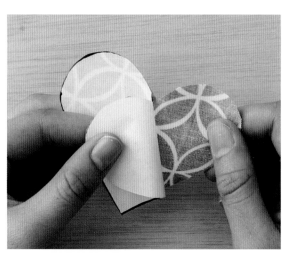

TIP If you are using solid fabrics that do not have obvious right and wrong sides, it will be easy to confuse the two after you peel away the freezer paper. To prevent this confusion, note which side should face up by attaching an adhesive note or pin to the right side.

5 Position the appliqués on the right side of the background fabric, with the right side of the appliqué fabric facing up. Using white glue, appliqué pins, or a needle and thread, baste the appliqués to the background fabric securely along all edges.

6 Stitch the appliqué edges using your choice of stitches, referring to Basic Machine-Appliqué Stitches (page 16). If you used thread to baste your appliqués in place, remove the basting stitches from the appliqué shapes now.

Embroidery-Finished Raw-Edge Appliqué

Like the ease and detail of raw-edge fusible appliqué but don't like the frayed edges? You can prevent them by chainstitching around the appliqués, encasing the raw fabric edges beneath a functional and attractive embroidered outline. This method takes time, but the handwork process is relaxing and enjoyable and results in an heirloom-quality product.

TIP I like to work with a hoop that is 7″ in diameter because it is easier to maneuver. Don't worry if the entire appliqué does not fit within the hoop. You will be outlining only a portion of it at a time, and you can always adjust the hoop as you go.

1 After machine stitching the appliqué to the background fabric, place the appliquéd piece in an embroidery hoop with the right side facing up.

2 Thread a needle with 3 strands of 6-stranded embroidery floss. Use approximately 18″ lengths of floss, as longer lengths will tend to fray as you stitch. Knot the end of the floss and then bring the needle from the wrong side of the appliqué piece to the right side, just adjacent to the edge of the appliqué.

3 Insert the needle back down into the fabric through the same hole you came up through or very close by. Pull the needle to the back of the fabric, but do not pull the thread all the way through. Instead, leave a large loop on the right side of the fabric.

4 Bring the needle back up to the right side of the fabric about ¼˝ away from the first hole, again in the background fabric adjacent to the appliqué. Insert the needle through the loop of thread you left on the right side of the fabric and pull taut to complete a chain stitch.

5 Repeat around the contours of the appliqué.

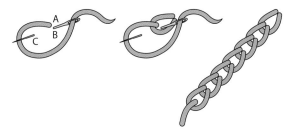

6 When you reach the final stitch, bring the needle to the right side of the fabric, thread beneath the head of the first chain stitch, and then insert back down through the hole you came up in. This creates the look of an unbroken chain and anchors the final stitch.

7 Secure the thread on the back of the piece by knotting or by weaving a 2˝ length through the back side of the stitches.

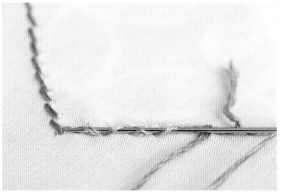

CONFETTI PILLOW

by Vanessa Christenson

Confetti Pillow by Vanessa Christenson

Finished size: 13″ × 13″

THIS PROJECT FEATURES:

- Raw-edge appliqué
- Fusible appliqué
- Machine stitching
- Appliqué-as-you-quilt

This fun quilted pillow will make any bed or chair feel like it's in the middle of a party with its cute confetti-falling-from-the-sky feel.

VANESSA CHRISTENSON

Photo by Kristy Honkomp, Studio K Squared

Vanessa Christenson is a blogger, quilter, and pattern designer known for her original sense of style and unique take on traditional motifs. Vanessa began blogging while her husband was deployed, as a means of keeping in touch, but it wasn't long before others took notice of the projects on her website.

One of her first opportunities to gain increased exposure was her participation as a chef for the Moda Bake Shop, sponsored by Moda Fabrics. Since then her designs have been featured in numerous magazines, including *Stitch*, *Quilty*, *Quilts and More*, and Fons and Porter's *Love of Quilting*. She is the author of *Make It Sew Modern* and has contributed quilt designs to numerous compilation books.

Vanessa is an in-demand public speaker and also has been featured on television and web-based media outlets such as *Quilting Arts* with Pokey Bolton, Fons and Porter's *Love of Quilting*, and Craftsy. She released her first Moda fabric line and Aurifil thread collection, Simply Color, in 2012, and is working on more.

Vanessa also is a BERNINA Ambassador and a contributor to BERNINA's *We All Sew* blog.

Vanessa is quick to point out that her most important role is as a wife and a mother to her husband and four children.

Vanessa's designs, projects, and patterns can be found on her website, vchristenson.com.

Confetti Pillows, 13″ × 13″, designed, made, and quilted by Vanessa Christenson, 2014

MATERIALS

The following materials are for 1 pillow.

TIP If you can't find ombré fabric, you can substitute five different solid fabrics in different values of the same color. Try to choose fabrics that will create an attractive gradient from light to dark.

- **Ombré fabric:** ¼ yard for appliqués

- **Linen:** ½ yard for background and pillow backing

- **Lightweight fusible web, 15″ wide:** ⅓ yard

- **Fusible batting:** 14″ × 14″ square

- **Muslin or woven interfacing:** 14″ × 14″ square

- **14″ × 14″ pillow form**

- **Removable fabric marker**

- **Thread to match background fabric**

TIP Vanessa always uses a slightly larger pillow form than the pillow cover so it fits full and snug.

Cutting

Refer to Preparing the Appliqués (page 28) and the Confetti Pillow pattern (pullout page P1) for directions on cutting the appliqués.

From the linen:

- Cut 1 square 14″ × 14″ for the pillow front.

- Cut 2 rectangles 14″ × 10″ for the pillow back.

From the fusible web:

- Cut 5 rectangles 3″ × 9″.

Preparing the Appliqués

1 Using the Confetti Pillow pattern (pullout page P1), trace dots onto the paper side of the fusible web. You'll be able to fit approximately 12 circles on each rectangle.

2 Following the manufacturer's instructions, fuse each rectangle onto the wrong side of the ombré appliqué fabric, placing the rectangles so that you have some circles from each shade in the fabric.

3 Cut out all the dots on the traced lines. Remove the paper backing from the dots.

4 Referring to the project photo and the appliqué placement diagram, arrange the dot appliqués randomly on the right side of the 14˝ × 14˝ background square with the lightest shade at the top and the darker shades toward the bottom. The spacing between the dots should range from very wide with the lightest dots to close together with the darkest dots. Overlap some of the dots.

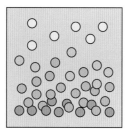

Appliqué placement

> **TIP** You will have more dots than you need, but more is better than not enough for this project.

5 When you are satisfied with the layout, pin each dot in place. Use an iron to fuse the dots to the background, following the manufacturer's instructions and remembering to remove the pins as you go.

Appliquéing-as-You-Quilt

1 Layer the pillow top, fusible batting, and muslin or woven interfacing as if you were making a quilt. Use an iron to fuse according to the manufacturer's instructions.

2 Quilt the pillow top with an allover pattern, which will also secure the appliqués.

Finishing

Referring to Finishing a Pillow (page 155), use the finished pillow front and the linen pillow backing rectangles to assemble the pillow cover.

Vanessa's Appliqué Tips

I really like the turned-edge appliqué look. Whenever possible I use this method for larger circles or petals:

1. Draw the appliqué shape on the back of the fabric.

2. Place the fabric, right side down, on a piece of lightweight fusible interfacing such as 880F Sof-Shape (by Pellon).

3. Sew on the drawn line of the appliqué shape.

4. Cut out the shape ⅛˝ from the sewn line. Clip around the seam for curved pieces so the curved areas will lie nicely.

5. Make a small slit in the interfacing and turn the piece inside out, gently pressing the shape with your fingers.

6. Now you have a shape that you can iron into place on the background fabric and then finish with machine or hand appliqué.

MIGRATIONS QUILT SAMPLER
by Shannon Brinkley

Migrations Quilt Sampler by Shannon Brinkley

Finished size: 34″ × 16″

THIS PROJECT FEATURES:

- Piecing
- Needle-turn appliqué
- Raw-edge appliqué
- Fusible appliqué
- Embroidery-finished appliqué
- Machine stitching
- Hand stitching

For this quilt, I decided to make a fun sampler. The Flying Geese block is a classic, a favorite of both traditional and modern quilters. I wanted to show that iconic design using several different quiltmaking techniques.

Starting on the left with the neat, classic block, the abstractly shaped geese gradually evolve into a more literally shaped "scrappy" goose.

The basic pattern is quick and simple, allowing the quilter to slow down for some fun detailed work, if desired, as well as try out four different techniques!

Photo by Matt Brinkley

SHANNON BRINKLEY

Shannon Brinkley is an elementary teacher turned quilt designer and author. A lifelong crafter, Shannon hopped from hobby to hobby (weaving, cross-stitch, knitting, garment sewing, and other crafts) as a girl but began quilting in college, where she fell completely in love with the craft. Inspired by her love of fabric and texture, Shannon wrote the book *Scrappy Bits Appliqué*, in which she puts a scrappy twist on traditional raw-edge appliqué techniques by collaging a variety of fabrics, vintage and new, with different colors, tones, and patterns to create a really interesting and unique texture. Her techniques are perfect for beginners and experienced quilters alike, as the steps are quick and easy to grasp and, once learned, offer a wide variety of creative possibilities.

Shannon lives in Austin, Texas, with her loving husband, Matt; wonderfully creative son, Davin; sweet pup, Piper; and surly kitty, Emily. Find out more about Shannon and her work at thebottletree.net.

Migrations Quilt Sampler, 34″ × 16″, designed, made, and quilted by Shannon Brinkley, 2014

MATERIALS

Unless otherwise noted, all measurements refer to 40″-wide 100% cotton quilting fabric.

- **Background fabric:** 1 yard

- **Various prints and/or solids:** 3 different scraps at least 7″ × 13″ for Geese 1, 2, and 3

- **Various yellow fabric pieces:** ½ yard total for Goose 4 (if using scrappy option) *OR* 1 scrap at least 7″ × 13″ for Goose 4 (if not using scrappy option)

- **Batting:** 24″ × 42″

- **Backing:** 1¼ yards *OR* ¾ yard if fabric has a usable width of 42″

- **Binding:** ⅓ yard

- **Lightweight fusible web, 15″ wide:** 2 yards

- **Freezer paper**

- **Cotton thread:** to match Goose 2 for needle-turn appliqué

- **Invisible thread for machine appliqué and 6-stranded cotton embroidery floss:** to match Goose 3 or machine-embroidery thread to match Goose 3

- **Machine-embroidery thread:** to match Goose 4

NOTE: The finished quilt features a "scrappy" Goose 4, made using Shannon's signature technique. To learn more about her method, see Resources (page 157) for information about her book, Scrappy Bits Appliqué.

Cutting

Refer to Appliquéing the Geese *(page 33) and the* Migrations Quilt Sampler *patterns (pullout page P1) for directions on cutting the appliqués.*

From the background fabric:

- Cut 1 strip 12½˝ × width of fabric.

  Subcut 1 strip 12½˝ × 24½˝.

  From the remainder, subcut 2 squares 6½˝ × 6½˝.

- Cut 3 strips 2¼˝ × width of fabric for the borders.

  Subcut 1 strip in half to form 2 border strips 2¼˝ × approximately 20˝.

From the Goose 1 fabric:

- Cut 1 rectangle 6½˝ × 12½˝.

Piecing Goose 1 and the Background

1 Fold the 2 background squares in half on the diagonal. Press to create guidelines for stitching; unfold.

2 Place a background square on the left side of the Goose 1 rectangle, right sides together. Make sure the diagonal crease is oriented as shown. Align the raw edges and pin in place.

3 Stitch on the crease. Trim the excess fabric to a ¼˝ seam allowance. Press the seam open.

4 Repeat Steps 2 and 3 for the right side of the 6½˝ × 12½˝ rectangle. Press the seam open.

5 Fold the 12½˝ × 24½˝ background piece in half lengthwise; then fold in half again. Then fold in half widthwise; press to create creases and unfold. Your fabric will be marked into 4 equal columns and 2 rows. The creases are guidelines

for the placement of the Geese 2, 3, and 4 appliqués.

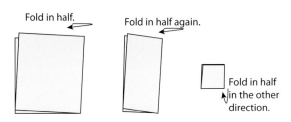

Fold in half.

Fold in half again.

Fold in half in the other direction.

6 Sew the Goose 1 block as shown to the left end of the creased back-ground piece. Press the seam open. Be sure the guideline creases are still visible.

7 Sew short border strips to the left and right sides of the quilt sampler.

Press the seams open. Trim the excess fabric. Sew the long border strips to the top and bottom. Press the seams open. Trim the excess fabric.

Appliquéing the Geese

Goose 2

Referring to Needle-Turn Appliqué (page 43), the appliqué placement diagram, and the Goose 2 pattern (pullout page P1), prepare the appliqué and then baste and stitch the appliqué to the background. *Note: This pattern has not been reversed because it is for needle-turn appliqué. If you choose a different appliqué method, you may need to reverse it.*

Goose 3

Referring to Fusible Raw-Edge Appliqué (page 19), the appliqué placement diagram, and the Goose 3 pattern (pullout page P1), prepare and stitch Goose 3 to the background fabric.

TIP : This pattern is reversed for use with fusible web. Shannon used Casey's technique for Embroidery-Finished Raw-Edge Appliqué (page 23) to chain stitch the edges of this goose.

Goose 4 (Scrappy Goose)

TIP : Shannon used the techniques in *Scrappy Bits Appliqué* to make a fabric collage. You can also use a piece of solid or print fabric for Goose 4. If you make a scrappy goose, remember to stitch down the pieces of the fabric collage when you stitch the outer edges of the goose.

1 Referring to Nonfusible Raw-Edge Appliqué (page 21) and the pattern for Goose 4 (pullout page P1), prepare Goose 4 by pressing the freezer paper pattern onto the *right* side of the fabric. Cut out and baste Goose 4 to the background. This goose will cover the last 2 columns created by the folds. *Note: This pattern has not been reversed.*

2 Machine stitch or embroider around the edge of Goose 4. Shannon machine appliquéd this goose using a satin stitch.

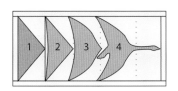

Appliqué placement

Finishing

1 Refer to Finishing a Quilt (page 150) to layer, baste, and quilt as desired.

2 Refer to Binding (page 151) or use your preferred method to make and attach the binding.

3 If you plan to hang the quilt, refer to Hanging Sleeves (page 154) to add a sleeve.

> ### Shannon's Appliqué Tips
>
> *Depending on the method you use, appliqué can be much quicker and simpler than piecing. Appliqué can also be an opportunity to slow down and put a lot of love and attention into a project. I like to strike a balance by designing patterns that are simple and efficient so the quilter is able to slow down during the fun parts, like fabric selection, or perhaps some hand embroidery or intricate quilting.*

Photo by John Lessard

Kevin Kosbab

Quilt designer and author Kevin Kosbab uses many different appliqué techniques, but needle-turn is his favorite for its relaxing nature and portability. He also enjoys the slightly imperfect look of needle-turn appliqué because it shows the hand of the maker.

To choose the technique for a project, he takes into account both the design and the way the piece will be used. For a children's quilt for his recent book *The Quilter's Appliqué Workshop* (2014), he chose raw-edge appliqué stitched with a sturdy zigzag that will withstand intense usage. For a wallhanging, in contrast, he might turn to a different technique such as needle-turn. He also considers how the stitching can accentuate the design of the quilt, adding dense satin stitching to outline shapes, for example.

Kevin notes that appliqué opens new design possibilities for modern quilters.

"Improvisational piecing is so prevalent in modern quilting … and appliqué always has an element of that to it and lends itself to improvisation even more than piecing does," Kevin says.

Kevin encourages people to embrace appliqué because it is fun, a sentiment that shines in his playful quilts. You can learn more about Kevin's work at his website, feeddog.net.

Peacocks on Parade, 46″ × 46″, designed, made, and quilted by Kevin Kosbab, 2011
Photo by Kevin Kosbab

In the Kitchen, 49½″ × 53½″, designed, made, and quilted by Kevin Kosbab, 2013
Photo by Kevin Kosbab

GINKGO BED RUNNER

by Casey York

Finished size: 80″ × 28″

THIS PROJECT FEATURES:

- Raw-edge appliqué
- Fusible appliqué
- Machine stitching
- Embroidery-finished appliqué

I love bed runners. They're a great quilted project to dress up your bed without having to make a full-size quilt. Moreover, their smaller size makes them easier to quilt. If you wish to make a full quilt, simply follow the placement diagram but enlarge the background fabric to measure the final quilt size.

Photo by Randall Kahn

CASEY YORK

Casey York is a quilt designer and author known for her bold, minimalist appliqué quilts. For more information about Casey, see About the Author (page 159).

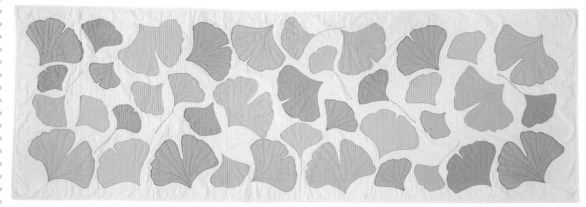

Gingko Bed Runner, 80″ × 28″, designed, made, and quilted by Casey York, 2014

MATERIALS

Unless otherwise noted, all measurements refer to 40″-wide 100% cotton quilting fabric.

- **White:** 2½ yards for background
  OR 1 yard if fabric is 90″+ wide

- **Yellow:** ½ yard for leaves

- **Gold:** ½ yard for leaves

- **Yellow green:** ½ yard for leaves

- **Acid green:** ½ yard for leaves

- **Kelly green:** ½ yard for leaves

- **Backing:** 2½ yards

- **Batting:** 88″ × 36″

- **Binding:** 1 yard for bias binding
  OR ⅝ yard for straight-grain binding

- **Double-sided lightweight fusible web, 15″ wide:** 3 yards

- **Invisible thread**

- **6-stranded cotton embroidery floss:**
  1 skein to match each appliqué color

- **Removable fabric marker**

Cutting

Refer to Fusible Raw-Edge Appliqué (page 19) and the Gingko *patterns (pullout page P1) for directions on cutting the appliqués.*

TIP As you trace your patterns, also transfer the labels and color suggestions onto the paper backing of the fusible web. This way, you will have no confusion about which template to fuse to which appliqué fabric.

From the white fabric:
- On the lengthwise grain, cut a rectangle 28″ × 80″.

Assembling the Top

1 Refer to the appliqué placement diagram below to arrange the appliqués on the background fabric and fuse them in place.

2 Use invisible thread and a zigzag or blanket stitch to machine stitch around the edge of each appliqué.

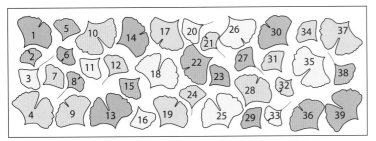

Appliqué placement diagram—Leave at least 1½˝ on all edges of the background fabric to allow enough room for the binding.

Embroidering the Appliqués

1 Finish the raw edges of the appliqués by encasing them beneath a line of hand embroidery. Refer to Embroidery-Finished Raw-Edge Appliqué (page 23). Use 3 strands of 6-stranded cotton embroidery thread in a color that matches each appliqué.

2 Using a removable fabric marker, transfer the stem pattern to the ends of leaves 3, 8, 12, 20, 21, 24, 27, 33, and 38 (pullout page P1). Note that the stem pattern is not reversed and should be transferred *as is* to the background fabric. Embroider the stems using a chain stitch and 3 strands of floss in a color that matches the appliqué fabrics.

Finishing

1 Refer to Finishing a Quilt (page 150) to layer, baste, and quilt as desired.

2 Refer to Binding (page 151) or use your preferred method to make and attach the binding.

3 If you plan to hang the quilt, refer to Hanging Sleeves (page 154) to add a sleeve.

Casey's Tips

Adding embroidery around your appliqués protects the raw edges and also lends them additional textural interest.

Although I usually prefer to use three strands of six-stranded floss in a color that matches my appliqué fabric, you can achieve wonderful results by using contrasting colors and different types and textures of thread, such as perle cotton.

Photo by Nate Watters

LUKE Haynes

Looking at LUKE Haynes's work, one is struck by the multilayered nature of the compositions, which often combine realistic-looking appliqué images with pieced backgrounds in contrasting colors. LUKE works from printed templates to layer different colors and values of fabrics, initially securing them with a glue stick. He then stitches down the raw edges of the appliqué pieces—some of which can be quite tiny—using a longarm quilting machine.

LUKE seeks to use his work to foster a dialogue about objects, materiality, and method. One of his first quilted series, titled Man Stuff, comprised objects often associated with masculinity but rendered in textiles, which Western society often considers feminine. He also likes to engage with the traditional division between "fine art" and "craft," arguing that these two camps should not be seen as oppositional and that "a lot more credence should be put into the intention of the maker."

The quilt is an ideal site for such a dialogue, considering that the object itself is rooted in its own utility and often made to be used. Asked whether he envisions his own quilts being used, LUKE admits that while each work is intended to be durable enough for use, he prefers the wider audience that his work can reach in a gallery as opposed to in a private collection.

To learn more about LUKE, visit his website at lukehaynes.com.

[Man Stuff #1]
Hammer, 84″ × 72″, designed, made, and quilted by LUKE Haynes (assisted by Jen Dombrowksi), 2006
Photo by
Nate Watters

[Clothes Portrait #1]
Cupcake, 36˝ × 60˝,
designed, made,
and quilted by
LUKE Haynes
(assisted by Angela
Lauer), 2013
Photo by
Nate Watters

TURNED-EDGE APPLIQUÉ

In turned-edge appliqué techniques, the edges of each appliqué are turned under, so that the exposed edge of the shape is actually a crease in the fabric rather than a raw edge left vulnerable to fraying.

Turned-edge appliqué techniques are the ones that come most readily to mind when one thinks of the history and traditions of appliqué. This is for good reason: the double layer of fabric that outlines each appliqué with turned-edge techniques makes for a somewhat sturdier product, with the additional advantage that the edges of the fabric can be left visible (that is, not encased beneath stitching) without the likelihood of fraying.

The lovely finished edges of turned-edge appliqué can be achieved in a variety of ways—some by hand and some using a sewing machine—but they do require a greater investment in preparation and time than raw-edge techniques. In needle-turn appliqué, the seam allowance is turned under as the appliqué shape is hand stitched to the background. In other turned-edge techniques, the edges of the appliqués are turned under and either creased with an iron or glued down before the shapes are sewn to the background. A secondary material such as freezer paper can be used to aid this process but often must be removed after stitching, requiring cutting the background fabric away from behind each appliqué.

These techniques can be divided into two basic categories: needle-turn appliqué, which is hand sewn, and machine-sewn techniques that require the seam allowances of each appliqué shape to be turned under prior to stitching. These instructions will guide you through the basics of each submethod, but be sure to read the directions and author tips for each of the projects in this section to get a more nuanced look at the various subtechniques that are at your disposal.

Needle-Turn Appliqué

In needle-turn appliqué, you turn under the edge of the appliqué as you stitch it to the background fabric. Loved and admired for its remarkable results, needle-turn appliqué is also perhaps the most feared of appliqué techniques. The process can be time-consuming and requires a considerable amount of practice to master. However, needle-turn appliqué can also be meditative and relaxing. Patterns are transferred to the right side of the appliqué fabric, so they do not need to be reversed.

1 Make a template for transferring the appliqué pattern to the fabric. Place a sheet of translucent template plastic on top of the pattern to be transferred and use a fine-tipped permanent marker to trace the pattern onto the plastic.

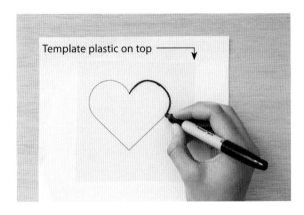

Template plastic on top

If you are making a plastic template from a pattern that has been reversed (for example, a pattern intended for fusible appliqué), flip the traced plastic template over and label the *opposite* side as the *right* side.

If you do not have template plastic, you can also use freezer paper. Lay the freezer paper, shiny side down, on top of the pattern and trace it. Press to temporarily adhere the freezer paper pattern to the *right* side of the appliqué fabric. If the pattern is reversed, trace the reversed pattern onto the *shiny* side of the freezer paper,

cut out the template on the traced lines, and then adhere the template to the *right* side of the appliqué fabric. Alternatively, trace the reversed pattern as is and adhere the freezer paper to the *wrong* side of the appliqué fabric.

TIP Whether you should use template plastic or freezer paper will depend on how often the appliqué shape will repeat in your overall design. If you are working with a shape that will repeat often, it can save time to make a plastic template. If you are working with a design that has many shapes that occur only once each, freezer-paper templates will work fine and be more economical.

2 Cut out the template on the traced lines.

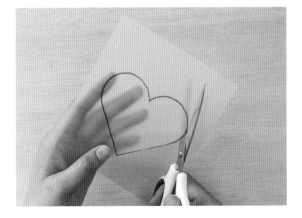

3 Using a removable fabric marker, trace around the template onto the right side of the fabric to indicate the stitching line. If you are using freezer-paper templates, iron them to the right side of the fabric and then trace around the templates to make guidelines for your stitching.

4 Cut out the appliqué shape, leaving a ⅛˝–¼˝ seam allowance outside the traced edge of the template. With experience, you will find your preferred seam allowance and will be able to easily eyeball it, but feel free to start with a wider seam allowance and mark it at first. If you are using a freezer-paper template, peel away the paper after cutting out the shape.

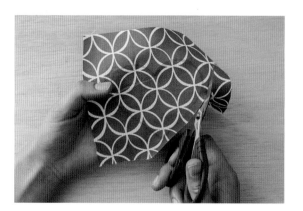

5 Clip the seam allowance along inside curves and points, stopping just before the traced stitching line. Do not clip outside curves. You may prefer to wait to clip the seam allowance until the appliqué is basted in place and you are about to stitch that area. You may also want to finger-press along the traced line to make it easier to needle-turn the shape later.

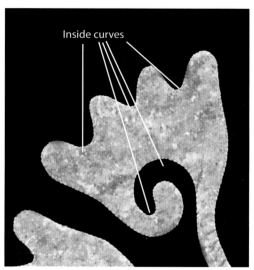

6 Baste the appliqué to the background fabric, with right sides up. Refer to Basting Appliqués (page 15). Make sure your pins, basting stitches, or glue are at least ¼″ *inside* the traced stitching line, as you will need this fabric to be free in order to turn under the seam allowance when stitching it down.

7 Thread a hand-sewing needle with no more than 15″ of fine thread that matches the appliqué fabric color. Silk or 50-weight cotton are good choices. Knot the end of the thread.

8 Start stitching on a relatively straight section of the appliqué. Bring the threaded needle up from behind the appliqué fabric to the top of the appliqué fabric on the traced stitching line; the starting knot will be secured between the appliqué fabric and the background fabric.

Contrasting thread is used here for visibility; for best results, use a thread that matches your appliqué fabric.

9 Use the tip of the needle to push the seam allowance under the appliqué with a sweeping motion.

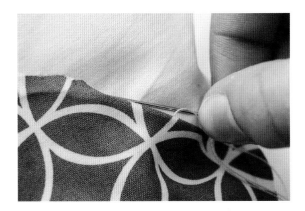

10 Insert the needle down into the background fabric directly adjacent to the point at which it emerged from the appliqué fabric. The stitch should be barely visible. Travel underneath the background fabric and bring the needle back up about ⅛″ away, catching a few threads of the folded appliqué fabric edge, to complete a stitch.

11 Repeat Steps 9 and 10 around the entire contour of the appliqué. (If an area will be covered by another area, you don't need to appliqué it down.) Use the tip of the thumb on your non-needle hand to hold the turned-under allowance in place. On straight edges, you will be able to turn under a longer section at once, but on curves you may need to turn under a bit of the allowance with each stitch. Remember to clip the seam allowance on inside points and inside curves if you didn't do this before basting.

TIP When stitching up to an inside point, gradually stitch farther into the appliqué as you approach the point, and then less far as you stitch away. This helps keep the inside point from fraying at the clip.

12 When you have finished, bring the needle and thread to the back of the background fabric and make a knot.

Alternative Turned-Edge Techniques

In these methods, the seam allowance is secured behind the appliqué before stitching. These methods are most often used with machine stitching, but some quiltmakers use these techniques in preparation for hand appliqué as an alternative to needle-turn.

There are many ways to prepare turned-edge appliqués, and each has its proponents. The best strategy is to keep trying different methods until you find one that suits your personal style and project.

Freezer Paper and Glue Technique

This method uses a washable glue stick to secure the seam allowance of each appliqué to a freezer-paper template. The freezer paper stays in the appliqué during stitching and must be removed after stitching is complete. Use a narrow machine stitch with this method to ease the removal of the freezer paper.

TIP The following instructions refer to freezer paper, but Wash-Away Appliqué Sheets can be substituted. Like freezer paper, wash-away paper fuses to the wrong side of the appliqué fabrics, which means that you can use it to transfer appliqué patterns to fabric. Unlike freezer paper, however, it dissolves in water instead of needing to be removed after stitching. Refer to *Beach Huts* (page 66) for more details about a project made with this product.

1 Place a sheet of freezer paper with the shiny side down over the reversed pattern to be transferred and use a pencil or fine-tipped permanent marker to trace the pattern onto the *dull* side of the freezer paper. As templates cannot be reused to make multiple appliqués with this method, make a template for each appliqué piece in the project.

Shiny side down

2 Cut out the freezer-paper template on the traced lines.

TIP If you need to make several copies of a freezer-paper template, you can save time by tracing the template onto one sheet of freezer paper, stapling that to the top of several more sheets, and cutting them all out at once along the traced lines.

3 Position the freezer-paper template on the wrong side of the fabric, shiny side down. Use an iron to adhere the paper temporarily to the fabric.

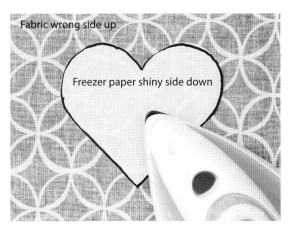

Fabric wrong side up

Freezer paper shiny side down

4 Cut out the appliqué shape, leaving a ¼˝ seam allowance outside the edges of the freezer-paper template.

5 Clip inside curves and points, stopping just before the edge of the freezer-paper template. Do not clip outside curves.

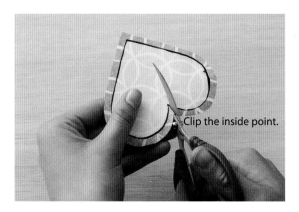
Clip the inside point.

Do *not* clip outside curves.
Clip inside curves.

6 Place the appliqué on your work surface with the freezer-paper side facing up. Working only an inch or so at a time, swipe a washable glue stick from the paper template toward the edge of the seam allowance.

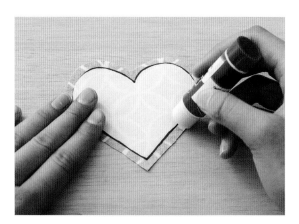

TIP Paintbrushes and rubber-tipped color applicators can also be used to apply glue from a glue stick to the seam allowance of the appliqué. See Materials (page 8).

7 Use your fingers to carefully fold the seam allowance toward the freezer paper along its edge, pressing to stick in place and achieve a sharp crease. Periodically turn the appliqué over to check that the edges are smoothly curved. Do not fold under the edges of any areas that will be overlapped by another appliqué shape.

TIP Glue sticks can become gooey when they get warm. To combat this, keep your capped glue sticks in the refrigerator or freezer between uses.

8 When all the edges have been turned under, press the appliqué from the right side with a dry iron. Protect your ironing surface from any glue residue by using an appliqué pressing sheet or Silicone Release Paper.

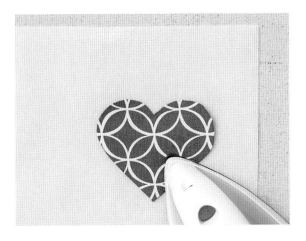

9 Baste the appliqué to the background fabric using your preferred method. Machine stitch in place using a very narrow stitch that just catches the folded edge of the shape. See Basic Machine Appliqué (page 14).

10 Turn the appliquéd piece over. Very carefully cut away the background fabric behind each appliqué to within ¼″ of the stitching line, taking care not to cut through the freezer paper or appliqué fabric.

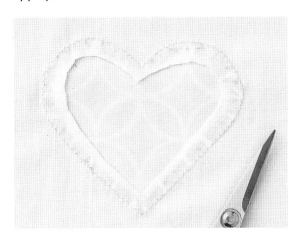

11 Use a spritz of water to soften the glue holding the freezer paper to the appliqué fabric. Using your fingers or a pair of tweezers, carefully peel the freezer paper away from the appliqué fabric and discard.

FREEZER PAPER AND STARCH TECHNIQUE

Although slightly fussier than the glue-prepared edge method, this method allows the freezer paper to be removed before the appliqués are stitched to the background. It also uses freezer-paper templates to guide the edge-turning process, but the edges are folded under using a starch solution and iron. If you are making a pattern in which the same appliqué shape occurs repeatedly, this method also allows you to trace fewer appliqué templates, as each freezer-paper template can be used more than once.

1 Place a sheet of freezer paper with the shiny side down over the reversed pattern to be transferred and use a pencil or fine-tipped permanent marker to trace the pattern onto the dull side of the freezer paper. For this method, it can be nice to have a stiffer template to turn the edges against. Place the sheet with the tracing on top of several more sheets, all with the shiny side facing down. Press to adhere the layers together. Cut out the freezer-paper template on the traced lines.

2 Follow Freezer Paper and Glue Technique, Steps 3–5 (page 48).

3 Place the appliqué on a pressing surface with the freezer paper facing up. Spray a good quantity of spray starch into a small container and use a paintbrush to apply it to the wrong side of the seam allowance, working about 1″ at a time.

4 Fold the seam allowances over the freezer paper while the starch is still damp and use a dry iron to press it in place. A mini iron can be useful for this step. Periodically turn the appliqué over to check that the edges are smoothly curved. Do not fold under the edges of any areas that are overlapped by another appliqué shape.

5 When all the edges have been turned under, turn the appliqué over and give it a final press to create sharp edges. Allow the appliqué to cool, and carefully peel away the freezer paper.

Stitch-and-Turn Appliqué

The stitch-and-turn method is great for turning the edges of simple shapes with gentle curves, and it requires no fussy ironing, gluing, or hand stitching to create an appliqué without exposed raw edges. You will need additional material as a facing, such as interfacing (fusible or nonfusible) or another lightweight fabric that will not be seen.

1 Transfer the reversed appliqué pattern provided onto the *wrong* side of the appliqué fabric. You can use a freezer-paper or plastic template for this.

2 Place the appliqué fabric against the facing with the *right* sides together and the tracing facing *up*; pin together. If you use fusible interfacing, the glue side should be facing the right side of the appliqué fabric (this allows you to fuse your flipped appliqués in place later instead of basting them).

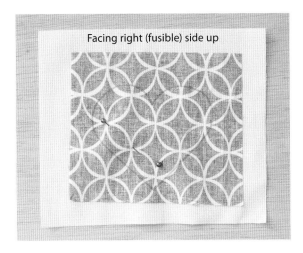

Facing right (fusible) side up

3 Using a straight stitch, machine stitch through both layers along the traced lines. Press to set the seam. *Note: If you are using a fusible interfacing as a backing, finger-press rather than using heat.*

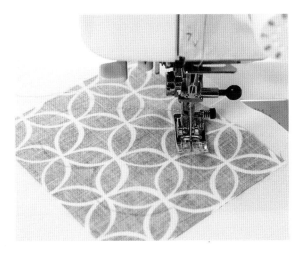

4 Cut out the appliqué shape through both layers, leaving a ⅛˝ to ¼˝ seam allowance outside the stitched lines. Clip the corners and curves.

5 Carefully cut a slit in the center of the facing and turn the appliqué right side out through the opening. Press the edges to smooth out the shape (if you have used a fusible interfacing, just finger-press).

6 Baste and machine appliqué in place using your preferred method.

FADING FOLIAGE

by Lynn Harris

Finished size: 87″ × 108″

THIS PROJECT FEATURES:

- Needle-turn appliqué
- Modern traditionalism

The October Foliage block was designed by Nancy Cabot and appeared in the November 11, 1936, issue of the *Chicago Daily Tribune*. Several years ago I saw Mary Shaffer's *October Foliage* quilt comprising appliqué blocks of red on muslin set alternately with plain muslin blocks and was intrigued by the secondary swirl pattern formed by the closely placed appliqué petals. I wanted to try the design with fabrics that might make this secondary pattern subtle. The fabrics used in *Fading Foliage* cause parts of the petals to disappear. Pairing three fabrics in each possible combination creates both boldly graphic blocks and more subtle blocks.

Fabric choice was very important to this quilt design. I started by choosing a large-scale print in two colors. The other two fabrics read the same as the two colors in the print. Pairing the large-scale print with either of the other two fabrics gives the illusion that part of the appliqué piece disappears or blends with the background.

Photo by Millie Carson

LYNN HARRIS

Lynn Harris has been sewing since she was nine years old. She learned to sew from her mother and was encouraged by her grandmother, who always told her that anything she made was the "most beautiful thing" she had ever seen. Lynn made many of her own clothes in middle and high school and completed her first quilt when she was twelve. She loves quilting with scraps and is the author of *Every Last Piece*, a book to help you use up your scraps. She has had quilts juried into the American Quilt Show in Paducah, the Modern Quilt Guild Showcase, and the QuiltCon show. She has had quilts published in *Pretty Little Mini Quilts* by Lark Books; *Minimal Quiltmaking* by Gwen Marston; and *Generation Q, Quilt*, and *Fat Quarterly* magazines.

Lynn lives in Michigan, where she grows vegetables and raises chickens with her husband and three amazing children. She enjoys many kinds of needlework and loves to knit, spin, embroider, and browse her collection of vintage children's books.

Lynn writes about her daily life and shares photographs of her creations on her blog, The Little Red Hen, at lynncarsonharris.com.

MATERIALS

Unless otherwise noted, all measurements refer to 40˝-wide 100% cotton quilting fabric.

- **Light blue solid or blender:** 1 yard for blocks and appliqués

- **Blue-and-black large-scale print:** 1 yard for blocks and appliqués

- **Black solid:** 7 yards for blocks, appliqués, and background

- **Backing:** 8¼ yards

- **Batting:** 95˝ × 116˝

- **Binding:** 1 yard

- **Freezer paper or translucent template plastic**

- **50-weight cotton thread or silk thread:** to match each appliqué fabric

- **Removable fabric marker**

Fading Foliage, 87˝ × 108˝, designed, made, and quilted by Lynn Harris, 2014

Cutting

Refer to Needle-Turn Appliqué (page 93) and the Fading Foliage *patterns (pullout page P2) for directions on cutting and preparing the appliqués. The patterns have not been reversed since this is a needle-turn appliqué project. You may wish to wait to clip the curves until the appliqués are being appliquéd in place.*

From the black background fabric:

- Cut 2 strips 15½" × width of fabric.

    Subcut 2 squares 15½" × 15½" for the block backgrounds.

    Subcut 7 rectangles 3" × 15½" for the sashing.

- Cut 1 lengthwise piece 108" × WOF.

    Subcut into 1 rectangle 24½" × 108" and 1 rectangle 8½" × 108".

- Cut 1 rectangle 40" × 108".

From the light blue fabric:

- Cut 2 squares 15½" × 15½".

From the blue-and-black large-scale print fabric:

- Cut 2 squares 15½" × 15½".

Making the Appliqué Blocks

1 Pair the Petal and Center appliqués with the 15½" × 15½" background squares as follows:

- Pair the black appliqués with the light blue and the print backgrounds.

- Pair the light blue appliqués with the black solid and the print backgrounds.

- Pair the print appliqués with the light blue and the solid black backgrounds.

2 Use the block placement diagram to arrange the Petal appliqués on the block backgrounds. Baste the Petal pieces to the background about ¼" inside the marked lines. See Basting Appliqués (page 15).

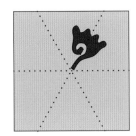

Block placement

3 Refer to Needle-Turn Appliqué (page 43) to appliqué the Petals to the background.

TIP When stitching this Petal shape, clip only once between the lobes of the Petals. The give of the bias edge will create a smooth curve.

4 Baste and appliqué the circles to the centers of the appliquéd squares, covering the ends of the Petal appliqués.

Assembling the Quilt Top

1 Referring to the quilt assembly diagram, stitch the appliqué blocks together with 3″ × 15½″ sashing strips between pairs and at each end of the row. The resulting strip should measure 108″.

2 Sew the 24½″ × 108″ black rectangle to the right side of the strip of blocks.

3 Sew the 40″ × 108″ black rectangle to the left side of the row of blocks.

4 Sew the 8½″ × 108″ rectangle to the left side of the 40½″ rectangle.

Finishing

1 Refer to Finishing a Quilt (page 150) to layer, baste, and quilt as desired.

2 Refer to Binding (page 151) or use your preferred method to make and attach the binding.

3 If you plan to hang the quilt, refer to Hanging Sleeves (page 154) to add a sleeve.

Quilt assembly

Lynn's Tips

In turned-edge appliqué, the give of the fabric's bias edge will create smooth outside curves. For this reason, you do not need to clip the seam allowances on an outside curve.

Clip the seam allowance only on an inside curve, and clip with the grain. When stitching this petal shape, clip only once with the grain between the lobes of the petals.

BELLE THE SQUIRREL, Circa 1975

by Jenifer Dick

Belle the Squirrel, Circa 1975 by Jenifer Dick

Finished quilt size:
80½″ × 93½″

Finished block size:
11″ × 11″

THIS PROJECT FEATURES:

- Turned-edge appliqué
- Machine stitching
- Modern traditionalism

Belle the Squirrel is an old-school, 1970s-inspired quilt. It started with the idea that I wanted to make a squirrel quilt. I drew my squirrel appliqué based on a block designed in 1938 by Nancy Cabot called Papa Squirrel. Then I decided to give a nod to those wonderfully quirky 1970s quilts that threw any and all colors together, whether they clashed or not! I worked my appliqué on the machine with a zigzag stitch, not caring if it was perfect or not to further evoke the relaxed style of the 1970s.

I used a wide variety of bright solids and accent prints for the blocks. Then I set it together in an old-school straight set with a gray sashing to give it a hint of modern. The result is a perfectly imperfect 1975–2015 hybrid of a quilt!

Photo by Eleanor Dick

JENIFER DICK

Jenifer Dick began quilting in 1993, when on a whim she signed up for a beginning quiltmaking class. From that first stitch she was hooked. In 2001 she discovered appliqué, and it changed her quilting life. She has been speaking to guilds and teaching appliqué to quiltmakers ever since. She is the author of five quilting books, including *The Modern Appliqué Workbook*, and her work has been published in many other books and magazines. See more of her work at 42quilts.com and contact her at jenifer@42quilts.com.

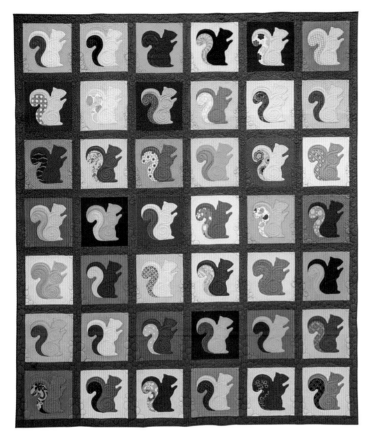

Belle the Squirrel, Circa 1975, 80½˝ × 93½˝, designed and made by Jenifer Dick, quilted by Kelly Cline, 2014

TIP

The more variety the better. If you don't want fabrics to repeat in your quilt, choose 42 warm and 42 cool solids. Or, choose 21 cool and 21 warm solids and use each twice in the quilt. You could also use two solids per squirrel instead of a solid/print combo. Let your instincts guide you, but don't overthink it! Some blocks that clash mixed with some beautifully coordinating blocks give this quilt its charm.

MATERIALS

Unless otherwise noted, all measurements refer to 40˝-wide 100% cotton quilting fabric.

- **Warm-color solids, such as reds, pinks, oranges, and yellows:** 42 different fat quarters for Body appliqués and backgrounds (choose 21 fat quarters if you don't mind colors repeating once in your quilt)

- **Cool-color solids, such as greens, blues, and purples:** 42 different fat quarters for Body appliqués and background squares (choose 21 fat quarters if you don't mind colors repeating once in your quilt)

- **Warm-color print or solid scraps, each approximately 4½˝ × 8˝:** 21 for Tail appliqués

- **Cool-color print or solid scraps, each approximately 4½˝ × 8˝:** 21 for Tail appliqués

- **Charcoal gray solid:** 3½ yards for sashing and binding

- **Backing:** 7⅝ yards

- **Batting:** 89˝ × 102˝

- **Freezer paper or Wash-Away Appliqué Sheets**

- **Washable glue stick**

- **Thread:** for machine appliqué in assorted colors

Cutting

Refer to Freezer Paper and Glue Turned-Edge Appliqué (page 46) and the Belle the Squirrel *patterns (pullout page P2) for directions on cutting the appliqués. The pattern is reversed for the freezer paper and glue technique.*

From each solid fat quarter:

- Cut 1 square 12″ × 12″ for the block back-grounds (42 total).

  Reserve the remaining fabric for the Body appliqués.

NOTE: If you are using 42 warm and 42 cool solid fat quarters, choose 21 warm colors and 21 cool colors and cut 1 square 12″ × 12″ from each; reserve the other 21 warm and 21 cool fat quarters for the Body appliqués.

From the charcoal gray:

- Set aside 1 yard for binding.
- Cut the remaining fabric into 32 strips 2½″ × width of fabric.

  From 12 strips, subcut 36 strips 2½″ × 11½″ for sashing.

  Piece the remaining strips and leftovers together end to end. Cut the resulting length into 7 strips 2½″ × 89½″ for the vertical sashing and side borders and 2 strips 2½″ × 80½″ for the top and bottom borders.

Making the Appliqué Blocks

1 Prepare 42 Body and Tail appliqués following the techniques in Freezer Paper and Glue Turned-Edge Appliqué (page 46). *Note: If you choose to use another appliqué method, test it first to make sure you are happy with the results and the finished orientation of the squirrels.*

NOTE: Do not turn under the edge of the Body appliqué that will be adjacent to the Tail appliqué (indicated on the patterns); the Tail appliqué will overlap the raw edge.

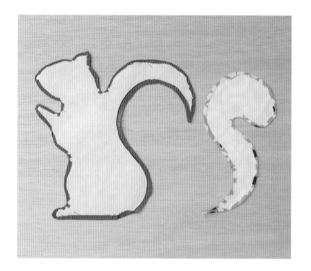

2 Pair up prepared Body and Tail appliqués—21 sets in warm colors and 21 sets in cool colors. Match each pair with a 12″ × 12″ background square of the opposite color scheme. (For instance, if your appliqués are cool colors, pair with a warm-colored background square.)

Choose a warm background with a squirrel in cool colors, like this aqua squirrel on a red background.

Or choose a cool background with a squirrel in warm colors, like this coral squirrel on a blue background.

3 Center each appliqué pair on a solid background square, arranging the Tail appliqué so that it overlaps the Body appliqué.

4 Referring to Basic Machine Appliqué (page 14), stitch each appliqué to the background using your favorite method.

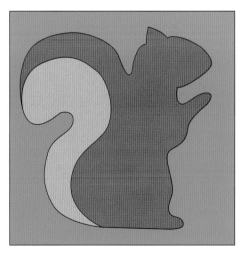

TIP Jenifer used a loose zigzag stitch in colored thread that either contrasted or matched depending on her mood, contributing to this quilt's homage to the rich, pop-art-infused colors of the 1970s. If she made a mistake stitching, she just backed up and did it again. This made some blocks look as if they were repaired later, adding further to the quilt's retro vibe.

5 If you used freezer-paper templates, remove the paper by cutting away the background fabric from the back of the block, being careful not to clip through to the appliqué. See Jenifer's Appliqué Tips (page 63) for more information on removing freezer paper.

6 Press the finished blocks and trim to 11½″ × 11½″.

Assembling the Quilt Top

1 Arrange the blocks in a 6 × 7 grid, alternating warm and cool backgrounds. Step back and make sure the colors are distributed evenly.

TIP The layout won't be perfect, so concentrate on the background colors and don't worry if the squirrel bodies clash a bit. Overthinking the layout will kill the retro feel and drive you insane!

2 Sew the blocks into columns with a 2½″ × 11½″ gray sashing strip between each pair of blocks. Press the seams toward the sashing.

3 Sew 89½″ vertical sashing strips between the columns and on each side. Press toward the sashing.

4 Sew the 80½″ horizontal strips to the top and bottom to finish the quilt top. Press.

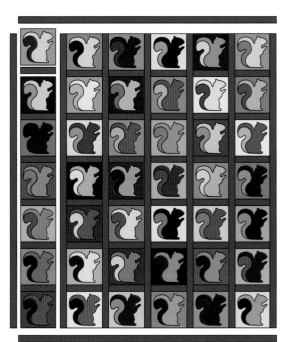

Quilt assembly

Finishing

1 Refer to Finishing a Quilt (page 150) to layer, baste, and quilt as desired.

2 Refer to Binding (page 151) or use your preferred method to make and attach the binding.

3 If you plan to hang the quilt, refer to Hanging Sleeves (page 154) to add a sleeve.

Jenifer's Appliqué Tips

I like the look of turned-edge appliqué, but I'm not very good at needle-turn! To get the shapes to look as perfect as I like, I use a freezer-paper method to prepare them. This also allows me to use a wide variety of threads and stitches to give the edges of my appliqué shapes a modern feel.

To remove the freezer paper, cut out the background behind the shape, leaving a ¼˝ seam allowance. Run the block under water and blot it with a terry cloth towel to remove the excess water. Let it sit for a few minutes. Gently tug on the diagonal of the block to loosen the freezer paper, and pull it out with your fingers. You can use tweezers to get the small bits that don't come out cleanly. Let the block thoroughly air-dry. Press. Trim to size.

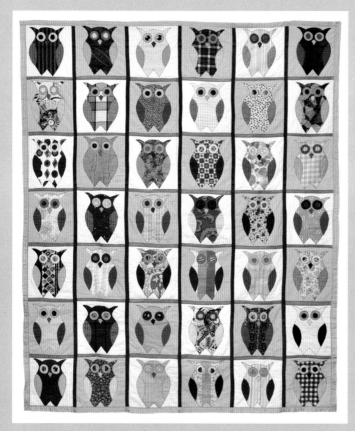

Owls, 66˝ × 79˝, unknown maker (Ohio), c. 1975. Photo courtesy of the Volckening Collection.

This wonderful pieced and appliquéd quilt, composed of cotton and cotton/synthetic blend fabrics, exemplified the quirky 1970s aesthetic that Jenifer channeled into her *Belle the Squirrel* project.

Photo by Bill Volckening

Photo by Sue Stubbs © CICO Books. Featured in Old Quilts, New Life *by Sarah Fielke (CICO Books, 2015)*

Sarah Fielke

Sarah Fielke has been sewing and appliquéing since she was a child, but she didn't use the needle-turn technique until she made a quilt for her son. Today, she describes this as her favorite type of stitching, both for its relaxing qualities and portability and for the freedom it gives her to design.

"I've always drawn, and once I figured out that I could make my drawings into sewing patterns, it changed everything," she says.

She tells her students, "The great thing about appliqué is that you can design your own [patterns]. Appliqué is freedom." She has developed a signature technique for teaching needle-turn appliqué that is fun and easy for beginners to learn.

"I love to make appliqué quilts but would hear so often from students and customers that hand appliqué was too hard for them or took too long. I set out to combat that!" More about her technique can be found in her books *Quilting from Little Things* (2011), *Hand Quilted with Love* (2013), and *Old Quilts, New Life* (2015).

Sarah's career in textiles began with a small business selling appliquéd baby and kids clothing and then evolved into a custom quiltmaking partnership. That led to her ownership of the fabric store that lent its name, Material Obsession, to her first two books with partner Kathy Doughty. Her style blends traditional appliqué designs with modern fabrics and colors to create a look that is distinctly her own.

You can see more of her work and learn more about Sarah at her website, sarahfielke.com.

I've Got Sunshine, 92½″ × 92½″, designed, made, and hand quilted by Sarah Fielke, 2014

Photo by Sue Stubbs © CICO Books. Featured in Old Quilts, New Life *by Sarah Fielke (CICO Books, 2015)*

BEACH HUTS WALL QUILT

by Allison Rosen

THIS PROJECT FEATURES:

- Turned-edge appliqué using wash-away appliqué paper (such as Wash-Away Appliqué Roll or Wash-Away Appliqué Sheets by C&T Publishing)

- Machine stitching

- Glue-prepared appliqué with Pro Arte Colour Applicators

- Appliqué-as-you-quilt

Wallhangings can add a lot of personality to your home and can be enjoyed by many if hung in a well-trafficked area rather than your bedroom! The details in this project add to its overall appeal, while the technique makes it a straightforward project—and it gets finished because while you appliqué, you're also quilting.

Photo by Joel Rosen

ALLISON ROSEN

Allison Rosen has been blogging and podcasting since 2007. Luckily, she discovered her love of appliqué right at the start of her quilting career and has been able to focus and grow her expertise in this technique. She offers patterns and kits on her website. Allison also has a graduate degree in accountancy and offers accounting services for the indie crafter through her Crafty Controller venture, something she finds extremely rewarding. She is a mama to nine-year-old twins and wife to an academic who still thinks she knits. Life is good. Learn more about Allison at her websites, withinaquarterinch.com and allisonrosen.com/the-crafty-controller/.

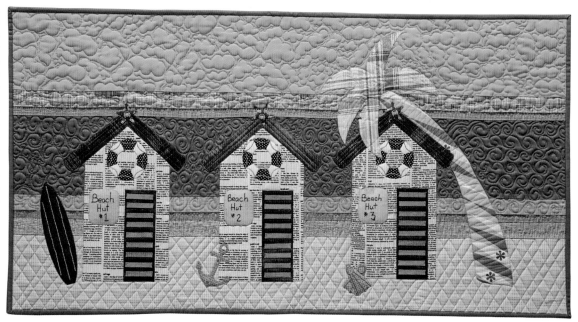

Beach Huts Wall Quilt, 36″ × 18½″, designed, made, and quilted by Allison Rosen, 2014

MATERIALS

Unless otherwise noted, all measurements refer to 40″-wide 100% cotton quilting fabric. Buy fabric cut across the width of fabric, not fat quarters, for the background fabric.

- **7 different assorted color fabrics:** ⅛ to ¼ yard each for background (Allison used ¼ yard each of light tan and light and dark solid turquoise, and ⅛ yard each of dark tan, green, and turquoise and pink prints)

- **Text fabric:** ⅓ yard for Huts

- **Stripe/print fabric:** 1 fat quarter for Palm Tree trunk

- **Assorted scraps:** for remaining appliqués

- **Backing:** ¾ yard

- **Batting:** 23″ × 44″

- **Binding:** ⅜ yard

- **Wash-Away Appliqué Roll, 14″ wide:** 1 roll (or 6 Wash-Away Appliqué Sheets, 8½″ × 11″; requires piecing the Palm Tree pattern)

- **6-stranded cotton embroidery floss:** 1 skein each of yellow, orange, and teal for appliqués

- **Perle cotton #16:** 1 skein black for Sign appliqués

- **1 stick purple wash-away school glue**

- **1 set Colour Applicators (2 applicators)**

- **1 nonstick appliqué pressing sheet**

- **Removable fabric marker**

- **Roxanne Glue-Baste-It or washable white school glue**

- **Invisible thread and/or thread to match appliqué fabrics**

Cutting

Note: Your background fabrics may be different colors. These are listed in order from top to bottom in the finished piece, so you can adjust your cutting to match.

Refer to Preparing the Appliqués (at right) and the Beach Huts *patterns (pullout page P1) for directions on cutting the appliqués from the assorted appliqué fabric and scraps.*

From aqua solid background fabric:

- Cut 1 rectangle 5½″ × 37″.

From pink print background fabric:

- Cut 1 strip 1½″ × 37″.

From green background fabric:

- Cut 2 strips 1″ × 37″.

From deep turquoise solid background fabric:

- Cut 1 strip 5½″ × 37″.

From light turquoise print background fabric:

- Cut 1 strip 1½″ × 37″.

From tan background fabric:

- Cut 1 strip 1½″ × 37″.

From light tan background fabric:

- Cut 1 strip 4½″ × 37″.

Assembling the Background

Stitch the background strips together along the long sides to form the background, placing the colors as shown in the background assembly diagram.

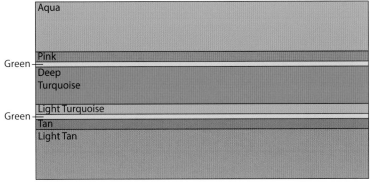

Background assembly

Preparing the Appliqués

1 Referring to the *Beach Huts* patterns (pullout page P1), trace each appliqué pattern onto the nonfusible side of the wash-away appliqué paper. The patterns are already reversed for this appliqué technique. Cut out the templates directly on the lines and fuse them to the wrong side of the various appliqué fabrics. Leave at least ½″ between pieces.

> **TIP** Use unexpected and fun prints to add whimsy and texture in unlikely places!

2 For the Hut appliqués, cut 3 rectangles 5⅞″ × 10″ from the wash-away appliqué paper. To shape the top of the huts, mark the center of a short end and 2⅛″ down from the corner on each adjacent long side. Use a rotary cutter and ruler to cut from the center of the short end to each mark. For the Door appliqués, cut 3 rectangles 2⅛″ × 5¾″ from the wash-away appliqué paper. Fuse to the wrong side of the corresponding appliqué fabrics.

3 Cut out the appliqué pieces from the fabric, leaving a ⅛˝ to ¼˝ seam allowance outside the edge of the paper templates.

TIP : Trim the seam allowance closer around points and curves to decrease the fabric bulk.

4 Place the nonstick appliqué sheet on your work surface to protect it. Using the Colour Applicators, paint a thin layer of glue from the purple glue stick onto the wrong side of each appliqué; make sure the glue completely covers the seam allowance and extends onto the paper template. Using the applicators, fold the seam allowances onto the paper and press to secure.

NOTE: Pay particular attention to overlapping shapes. Do not turn under any seam allowances that will be tucked under another shape. For example, do not turn under the seam allowances at the tops of the Huts because they will fit under the Roofs. Keep the side seam allowances on the white lifesaver pieces because those will fit under the red Lifesaver sections.

5 Move the appliqué to a clean area on your work surface between each application of glue to avoid getting excess glue on the right sides of your appliqués.

TIP : It helps to fold opposing edges over at the same time. For example, first fold the left side seam allowance and then the right side seam allowance; then fold the top and bottom seam allowances.

6 After all the edges have been glued under, turn the appliqué right side up and check that the edges are smooth.

7 Fold the pressing sheet in half and sandwich the appliqué between the 2 layers; press with a dry iron until the glue is no longer purple and turns a little brown.

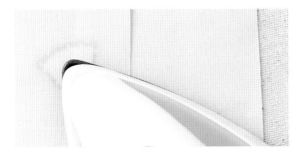

TIP
It is important to iron the appliqués until the glue is very dry, because this will make them easier to stitch through and will also keep your needle and machine cleaner.

Folding the pressing sheet in half prevents any glue from sticking to your iron or ironing surface. Use a Sharpie to mark the top side and always place your shapes glue side up on the lower side to prevent any excess glue from transferring from the sheet to other appliqué pieces by accident.

Preparing the Embroidered Appliqués

1 The Lifesavers, Swim Fins, Signs, and Surfboard appliqué shapes feature embroidered details. After you have folded over and glued all the edges and have used basting glue to assemble the Lifesavers, use a removable fabric marker to copy the embroidery lines from the patterns to the right side of the appliqués.

TIP
Use your own handwriting on the Signs to add a personal touch.

2 Use a backstitch (page 72) and 2 strands of embroidery floss to embroider along the traced lines on the Swim Fins, Surfboard, and Lifesavers. Use the black perle cotton to embroider the Signs.

BACKSTITCH

1 Bring the needle to the right side of the fabric and pull the thread through. Insert the needle into the fabric ¼″ away and complete a single stitch.

2 Bring the needle to the right side of the fabric about ¼″ from the point where the last stitch ended; pull the thread through.

3 Insert the needle into the fabric at the point where the last stitch ended; pull the thread through to complete the second stitch.

4 Continue repeating Steps 2 and 3 as needed.

TIP To cleanly pierce the wash-away appliqué paper and ensure that your embroidery accurately follows the traced lines, push the threaded embroidery needle through the front of the piece to make a hole and then remove the needle before you pull the thread through to the back. Use the hole you made to make the stitch. Continue making holes from the front of the appliqué piece, following the traced lines, to keep your stitches a consistent length and on the line.

Pierced hole

Assembling the Quilt Top

1 Following the quilt assembly diagram arrange the appliqués on the background fabric, making sure all the appliqués are at least 1½″ from the edges of the background fabric to leave enough room for trimming and binding. Note that some appliqués will overlap.

Quilt assembly

2 When you are satisfied with the layout, use white glue to baste everything in place. See Basting Appliqués (page 15).

3 Layer the quilt top, batting, and backing together and baste the layers. See Basting (page 150).

4 To secure the appliqués and quilt the wallhanging at the same time, use invisible or matching thread and a straight stitch to machine stitch the very edge of each appliqué to secure it to the background fabric. Be careful to catch the folded seam allowances to keep them from lifting.

> **TIP** If you are comfortable free-motion quilting, use a free-motion foot to attach the appliqué pieces. This will save you from having to continuously turn the whole piece under the needle.

5 Add texture to the appliqué pieces by stitching straight lines and zigzags on the Huts, Roofs, and Palm Tree trunk.

6 After each appliqué piece is secured and quilted, quilt the background.

Finishing

1 Trim to square up if needed. Allison trimmed her quilt to 36˝ wide.

2 Refer to Binding (page 151) or use your preferred method to make and attach the binding.

3 If you plan to hang the quilt, refer to Hanging Sleeves (page 154) to add a sleeve.

> **TIP** Use free-motion quilting to add interest to the background by adding clouds, waves, and other motifs.

Allison's Appliqué Tips

When I discovered the Colour Applicators in the fine arts department of an art supply store, I immediately thought, "I bet this would keep the glue off my hands!" I was right about that, but the extra benefits are also awesome. I can soften and spread the glue like icing on a cake and make it a smooth, thin layer that folds nicely. I can get into really tight spaces and leave them perfectly shaped because the applicators can get into crevices my fingers can't. The applicators are also heat-resistant, washable, and durable. And, finally, they make me happy!

Combine them with the wash-away appliqué paper and I'm in heaven—no more cutting the back of blocks to tear out freezer paper anymore!

Photo by Alexis Wharem

Carolyn Friedlander

Before she started quilting, Carolyn Friedlander was drawn to Hawaiian-style appliqué, in which fabric is folded and then cut to form radially symmetrical patterns. She describes seeing an exhibition of quilts in Hawaii and bringing home a book for her mother, only to rediscover that book years later after she had begun quilting herself. The influence of Hawaiian appliqué can be seen in the fold-and-cut construction of many of Carolyn's patterns and also is reflected in her method of designing, which often incorporates folded-and-cut paper "sketches."

Carolyn sees various appliqué techniques—like quilting techniques in general—as tools that can help us execute various ideas, noting that appliqué techniques "expand the range of what you can achieve stylistically."

Carolyn appreciates needle-turn appliqué because it requires minimal preparation of the appliqués before stitching. A proponent of the Slow Sewing movement, she also loves the peaceful, therapeutic nature of handwork.

Although her preferred technique could be seen as quite traditional in nature, Carolyn approaches it in a fresh way. Her background in architecture shines through in many of her designs, while her love of the natural surroundings of her native Florida informs others.

You can learn more about Carolyn in her first book, *Savor Each Stitch* (2014), and her website, carolynfriedlander.com.

Park Shams, 18˝ × 18˝, designed, made, and quilted by Carolyn Friedlander, 2014
Photo by Carolyn Friedlander

Botanics, various sizes, designed, made, and quilted by Carolyn Friedlander, 2013
Photo by Carolyn Friedlander

FALLING LEAVES

by Jenna Brand

THIS PROJECT FEATURES:

- Turned-edge appliqué
- Stitch-and-turn appliqué
- Hand stitching

Stitch-and-turn appliqué is a great technique for creating finished-looking pieces with standout design elements. The doubling of fabric creates a bold trapunto effect for the appliqué shapes. For this quilt, I turned to the paper-cutting work of artist Henri Matisse for inspiration. Graphic, abstract leaves are appliquéd onto a deep teal background, creating a fresh, modern look.

I provided three patterns for the leaves. These shapes can be repeated for all the leaves, or you can use them as inspiration to draft your own leaf patterns. For my quilt, I made each leaf different.

JENNA BRAND

Jenna Brand has been quilting for eight years, having been taught by her mother and a million Internet searches. Her quilts have been featured in the International Quilt Show and QuiltCon. Beyond sewing, Jenna is a wife, mother, and news editor. She blogs at jennabrand.com and can be followed on Instagram @howtobejenna.

Photo by Lisa Sutton

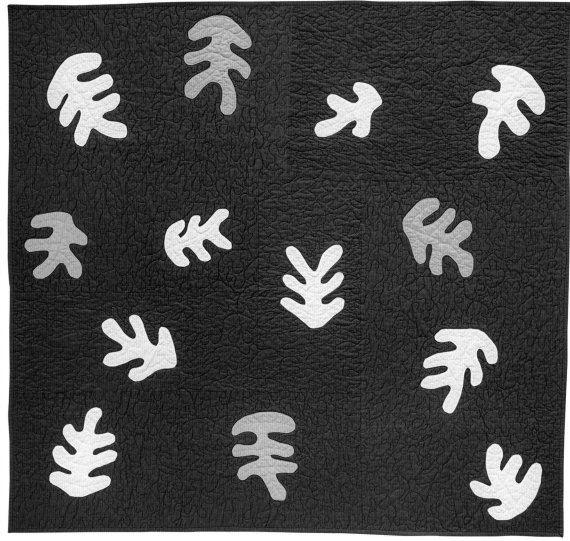

Falling Leaves, 65½˝ × 61½˝, designed, made, and quilted by Jenna Brand, 2014

MATERIALS

- **Blue solid:** 4 yards for background

- **White solid:** 1⅞ yards for leaf appliqués and appliqué facings

- **Yellow solid:** 1 yard for leaf appliqués and facings

- **Binding fabric:** ¾ yard

- **Backing:** 4 yards

- **Batting:** 74˝ × 69˝

- **Removable fabric marker**

- **Turning tool, such as Alex Anderson's 4-in-1 Essential Sewing Tool or a chopstick**

Cutting

Refer to Preparing the Appliqués (below) for directions on cutting the appliqués. Label the background pieces as you cut them.

From the blue background fabric:

- Cut 3 strips 21″ × width of fabric.

  Subcut a rectangle 33½″ × 21″ for Block A.

  Subcut a rectangle 15½″ × 21″ for Block B.

  Subcut a rectangle 17½″ × 21″ for Block C.

  Subcut 2 rectangles 16½″ × 21″ for Blocks I and J.

- Cut 1 strip 29½″ × width of fabric.

  Subcut a rectangle 13½″ × 29½″ for Block D.

  Subcut 1 rectangle 11½″ × 29½″ for Block G.

- Cut 2 strips 24½″ × width of fabric.

  Subcut 2 rectangles 12½″ × 24½″ for Blocks E and K.

  Subcut 2 rectangles 14½″ × 24½″ for Blocks F and H.

From the white solid:

- Cut 6 strips 10″ × width of fabric.

  Subcut 18 rectangles 12½″ × 10″.

From the yellow solid:

- Cut 3 strips 10″ × width of fabric.

  Subcut into 8 rectangles 12½″ × 10″.

Preparing the Appliqués

1 Set aside 9 white and 4 yellow rectangles for the top layer of the appliqués that will show.

2 The remaining white and yellow rectangles will be the facing, or bottom layer, of the appliqués. Use a removable fabric marker to trace a leaf shape onto the *wrong* side of each facing rectangle; this will be the bottom layer of the appliqué. Use the *Falling Leaves* patterns (pullout page P2) or draw your own leaf shapes directly onto the fabric.

> **TIP** If you are drafting your own leaf templates, keep the outer dimensions of the leaves to 8½″ × 11″.

3 Pair a facing rectangle (with a traced leaf) with a matching rectangle from Step 1, *right sides together*. Pin together with the traced line on top. Repeat to make a total of 9 white pairs and 4 yellow pairs.

4 Using a small straight stitch, sew directly on the traced line. Lift the presser foot and readjust the fabric layers in order to follow the curves of the leaf shapes. Secure the stitches by stitching forward and backward at the beginning and end.

5 Cut out the leaf shape from both fabric layers, leaving a ⅛˝ seam allowance.

6 From the facing side of the appliqué, cut a 1½˝–2˝ slit in the facing only. Be sure to cut through this layer only.

7 Turn the leaf right side out through the slit, using a turning tool to help push out the edges. Press the leaf flat from the top side.

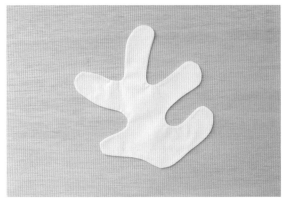

8 Repeat Steps 4–7 to make a total of 9 white leaves and 4 yellow leaves.

Assembling the Quilt Top

1 Arrange the blue background blocks according to the quilt assembly diagram (page 81).

2 Arrange the leaves on the background blocks until you are happy with the layout. Remember to place the leaves more than ¼˝ from the edges of the blocks to account for the seam allowance Pin the leaves in place.

If the background fabric shows through the slit in the back of the leaf, you can close the slit with a whipstitch or a small piece of fusible interfacing. Or, use a dense quilting design inside the leaf to hide the slit.

TIP

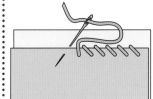

3 Using a blind stitch (at right), hand stitch the leaves onto each piece of background fabric.

4 Refer to the quilt assembly diagram to sew the appliquéd background blocks together in sections with a ¼″ seam allowance. Press. Sew the sections together to complete the quilt top.

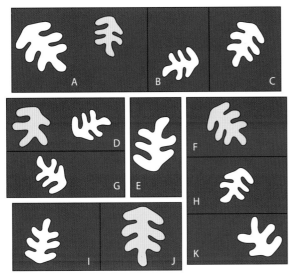

Quilt assembly

Finishing

1 Refer to Finishing a Quilt (page 150) to layer, baste, and quilt as desired.

2 Refer to Binding (page 151) or use your preferred method to make and attach the binding.

3 If you plan to hang the quilt, refer to Hanging Sleeves (page 154) to add a sleeve.

BLIND STITCH

1 Bring the needle and thread from the wrong side of the appliqué fabric to the right side (A).

2 Insert the needle down into the background fabric directly adjacent to where it emerged from the appliqué fabric (B).

3 Make a short stitch, about ⅛″ to ¼″, and bring the needle back to the right side of the background fabric (C). Insert the needle into the exterior fold of the appliqué fabric directly adjacent to where it emerged from the background fabric (D).

4 Make a short stitch through the appliqué fabric and bring the needle back to the right side.

5 Repeat Steps 2–4 along the contours of the appliqué.

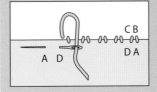

Jenna's Appliqué Tips

My favorite method for basting these appliquéd shapes onto the background is just to use a couple of pins.

Keeping the block on a hard surface that can be moved around, such a large hardcover book, often makes the hand-stitching element easier for me than trying to place the block inside an embroidery hoop.

REVERSE APPLIQUÉ

In many appliqué projects, the background fabric is just that—a background onto which a smaller piece of fabric is layered. In reverse appliqué, the "background" fabric is placed on top of the appliqué fabric, which shows through an opening cut in the background.

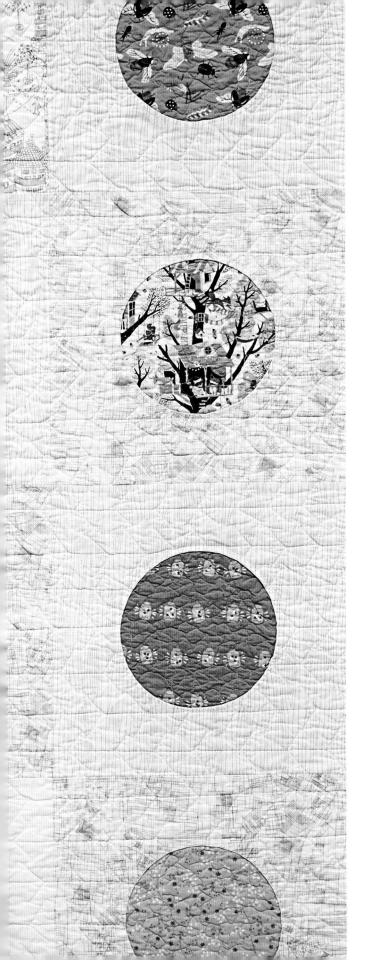

Basic Techniques

You can reverse appliqué using either raw-edge or turned-edge techniques.

As you will see in the projects that follow, you can choose from many appliqué techniques:

- Raw-edge

- Needle-turn

- Stitch-and-turn

- Improvisational stitching and cutting

In reverse appliqué, the fabrics are layered right side to wrong side. This makes sense when you remember that the layering occurs the same way in regular appliqué, but it can seem odd if you recently have been piecing, where you place right sides together.

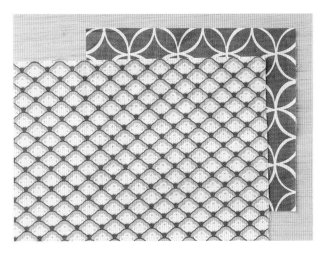

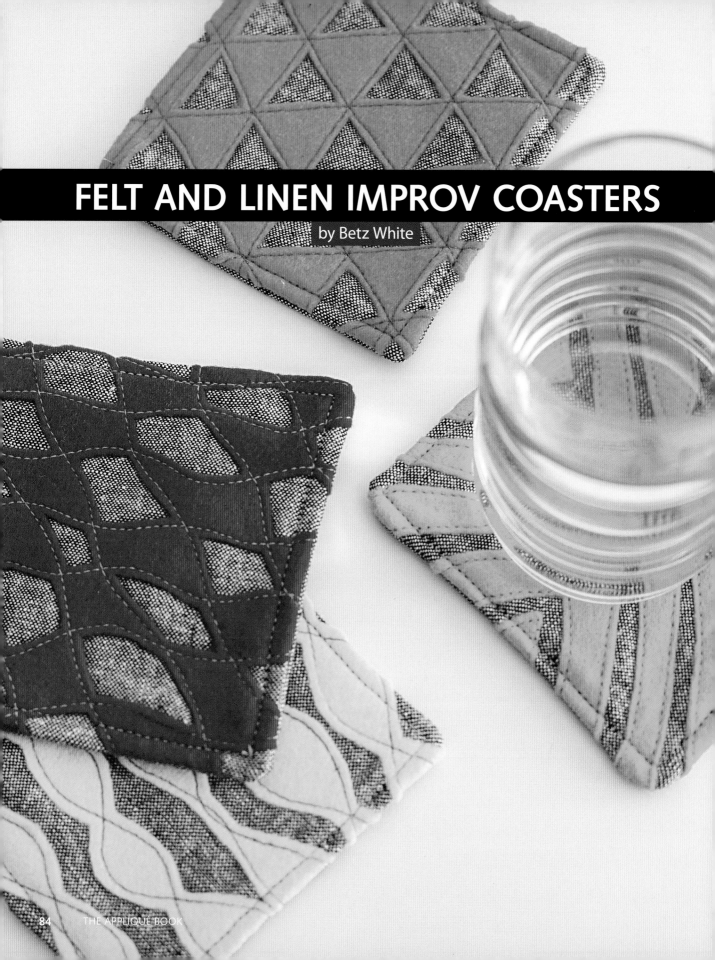

FELT AND LINEN IMPROV COASTERS

by Betz White

THIS PROJECT FEATURES:

- Reverse appliqué
- Machine stitching
- Improvisation

Improv coasters are fast and fun to make using a reverse appliqué technique. Stitch random lines and then cut out shapes of felt to reveal the base fabric underneath.

Photo by David C. White

BETZ WHITE

Designer and author Betz White has been sewing since her mother taught her as a young girl. A graduate in fashion design from the University of Cincinnati, Betz left her corporate career as a children's wear designer to stay home with her young children and pursue a new love: creating one-of-a-kind items from secondhand materials. Betz draws her inspiration from vintage shapes, elements of nature, and everyday objects. Her bold aesthetic combined with her education in apparel design results in unique patterns and projects for the modern sewer. Visit Betz at betzwhite.com and look for her newest book, *Present Perfect: 25 Gifts to Sew & Bestow.*

Felt and Linen Improv Coasters, 4″ × 4″, designed, made, and quilted by Betz White, 2014

MATERIALS

The following materials make 4 coasters.

- **Wool-blend felt:** 2 to 4 sheets (Felt is often sold in 6″ × 9″ or 8″ × 12″ sheets. Either size sheet will yield 2 of these coasters. Betz used 1 sheet each of pink, orange, green, and blue felt.)

- **Linen:** ¼ yard

- **Batting:** a scrap approximately 10″ × 10″

- **Thread to coordinate with felt colors**

- **Embroidery scissors**

Cutting

From the felt:

- Cut 1 square 4½″ × 4½″ from each color (4 total).

From the linen:

- Cut 8 squares 4½″ × 4½″.

From the batting:

- Cut 4 squares 4½″ × 4½″.

Appliquéing the Coasters

1 Layer a felt square on top of a linen square and pin. With coordinating thread, stitch lines across the square through both layers. Switch directions and stitch some more. You'll want to be sure to make "closed" shapes no smaller than ¼″ wide for the reverse appliqué.

<table><tr><td>

TIP Play with stitch designs with pencil and paper or by sewing on fabric scraps before you get started. (These designs are based on doodles that Betz makes while she's on the phone!) Try curvy, straight, or squiggly lines and then stitch in another direction to intersect the lines, so you can trim away the area within the stitch lines.

</td></tr></table>

2 With the tip of a sharp pair of embroidery scissors, snip a tiny hole in the top felt layer (not the linen layer underneath). Cut away an area of felt ⅛″ from the stitching lines. Continue cutting inside the stitched areas as desired.

3 Repeat to make 4 coasters.

Betz's Appliqué Tips

My favorite appliqué tip is to print or trace templates onto freezer paper. Freezer paper will temporarily stick to your felt or fabric, making it easy to cut out the shapes. It won't hurt your fabric, and it's also reusable! Just peel, reposition, and fuse again.

Finishing the Coasters

1 Layer another linen square for the backing onto the felt appliqué, right sides together. Place a square of batting on top. Pin the layers together.

2 Sew around the perimeter of the square with a ¼″ seam allowance, leaving a 2″ opening for turning on a side.

3 Clip the seam allowances at the corners and then turn the coaster right side out through the opening.

4 Press, folding in the seam allowances at the opening. Topstitch the perimeter of the coaster ⅛″ from the edge, closing the opening.

5 Repeat to make 4 coasters.

Girl with Side Eye, 10″ × 10″, stitched by Chawne Kimber, 2014
This cross-stitched artwork is Chawne's self-portrait.
Photo by Chawne Kimber

Chawne Kimber

Seeing the street-art-inspired self-portrait quilts of Chawne Kimber, one is struck by the possibilities that raw-edge appliqué open up to the quilter. A math professor and fiber artist, Kimber was introduced to textiles through cross-stitch, a skill that she learned from her godmother and continues to practice today. Although she sewed her own clothing and formal gowns throughout high school, and although Gee's Bend–style quilts were a fixture in her home growing up, Kimber did not begin quilting until 2005, when she took up the craft as a creative and therapeutic outlet during her tenure review.

Although she makes quilts durable enough for use, Kimber envisions her smaller appliqué quilts as display pieces that straddle the popular division between craft and fine art. She also grapples with larger ideas of censorship, language, relationships, and identity.

"It's [more] about the expression, not about the execution, although the execution is still important to me," she says. This desire to examine and explore deeper questions governs her style, in which photographs are simplified into graphic two-color images.

To create her appliqué quilts, Kimber begins with a photo that she manipulates until it is reduced to two colors. She then prints out the photo and stitches directly through the paper into multiple layers of fabric. The final step is to cut away the paper, as well as the top layers of fabric, revealing the contrasting fabric beneath. She often distresses the finished quilt in the washer and dryer to fray the exposed raw edges.

You can learn more about Chawne and follow her work on her website and blog, cauchycomplete.wordpress.com.

Self Study #1, 36″ × 36″, designed, made, and quilted by Chawne Kimber, 2012

Boys Don't Make Passes, 26″ × 35″, designed, made, and quilted by Chawne Kimber, 2014

ASTRID

by Lynn Harris

THIS PROJECT FEATURES:

- Reverse appliqué
- Needle-turn appliqué

I really enjoyed making this minimalist reverse-appliqué quilt out of Studio E's Peppered Cotton, a shot cotton made with two colors of thread. The warp threads are one color and the weft threads are another; the combination of these two thread colors gives a depth of color that changes when viewed from different angles. This particular fabric is wonderful for hand stitching and results in a very comfortable and drapey finished quilt.

I wanted the fabrics to do most of the talking in this quilt, so I kept the design simple. The block consists of a single slit that is reverse appliquéd to show a peek of the fabric layered below. Two under-fabric colors and three slit lengths provide the basic design elements of the quilt.

LYNN HARRIS

Lynn Harris is an award-winning modern quilter who has published quilts in many books and magazines. For more information about Lynn, see her profile in *Fading Foliage* (page 52).

Photo by Millie Carson

MATERIALS

Unless otherwise noted, all measurements refer to 40˝-wide 100% cotton quilting fabric.

- **Saffron solid:** ¼ yard for medium and small center openings

- **Paprika solid:** ⅛ yard for large center openings

- **Peacock solid:** 6⅛ yards for background *OR* 4½ yards if usable fabric width is at least 42½˝

- **Backing:** 5½ yards

- **Binding:** ⅞ yard

- **Batting:** 74˝ × 97˝

- **50-weight cotton thread or silk thread:** to match background fabric

Astrid, 66˝ × 87½˝, designed, made, and quilted by Lynn Harris, 2014

Cutting

From the peacock fabric:

- Cut 4 strips 3½˝ × width of fabric.

  Subcut 44 squares 3½˝ × 3½˝.

On the lengthwise grain:

- Cut 1 rectangle 18½˝ × 66˝.

- Cut 1 rectangle 24˝ × 66˝.

- Cut 1 rectangle 40˝ × 66˝.

From the saffron fabric:

- Cut 24 squares 3˝ × 3˝.

From the paprika fabric:

- Cut 12 squares 3˝ × 3˝.

Making the Appliqué Blocks

1 Use the *Astrid* pattern (pullout page P2) to mark the 3½″ × 3½″ peacock squares with a line centered diagonally on the right side of each square.

- 12 Block A squares: 3″ line
- 12 Block B squares: 2″ line
- 12 Block C squares: 1″ line

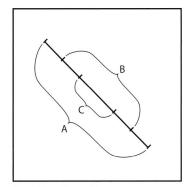

Astrid block marking

TIP Use dressmaker's tracing paper under the pattern to mark the fabric, or simply fold the pattern in half along the diagonal line and use the hatch marks to mark the A, B, or C slash line.

2 With sharp scissors, cut slits along the lines marked on the squares.

3 With right sides facing up, place each Square A on top of a paprika square, and each Square B *and* Square C on top of a saffron square. The raw edges will not align; make sure the smaller squares are centered beneath the peacock squares. Using a running stitch about ¼″ outside the slits, baste the squares together.

4 Use a needle-turn stitch (page 93) to reverse appliqué along the slits in the peacock fabric, turning the edges under so that the contrasting lower fabric peeks through. Use small stitches to secure the pointed ends of the top fabric because there will not be much fabric turned under there. Reverse appliqué all 36 blocks.

Assembling the Quilt Top

1 Using a ¼″ seam allowance and following the strip assembly diagram, stitch the appliqué blocks and background (non-appliquéd) blocks together. The finished strip should measure 66″ long.

Strip assembly

2 Sew the 18½″ rectangle to the top of the row of blocks. Sew the 40″ strip to the bottom of the row of blocks. Sew the 24″ rectangle to the bottom of the quilt top.

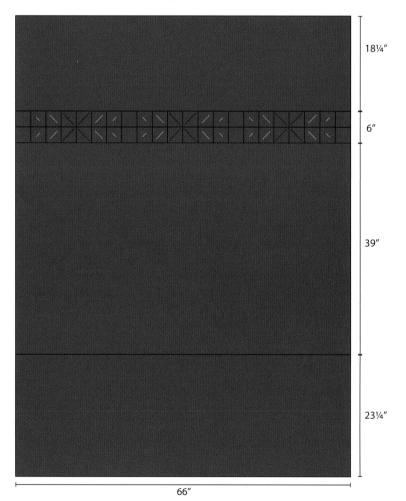

18¼″

6″

39″

23¼″

66″

Quilt assembly

Finishing

1 Refer to Finishing a Quilt (page 150) to layer, baste, and quilt as desired.

2 Refer to Binding (page 151) or use your preferred method to make and attach the binding.

3 If you plan to hang the quilt, refer to Hanging Sleeves (page 154) to add a sleeve.

Lynn's Appliqué Tips

For best results, press the fabrics well and try to keep the blocks flat and smooth while working on them. The edge is easier to turn under if it is still a crisp, unfrayed cut.

MOMENTS

by Rossie Hutchinson

Moments by Rossie Hutchinson

Finished quilt size: 80″ × 80″
Finished block size: 20″ × 20″

THIS PROJECT FEATURES:

- Reverse appliqué
- Stitch-and-turn appliqué
- Machine stitching

This is a simple block that lends itself well to showing off a collection of fabric. This design came about because of my love of Teagan White's fabrics—we see her Fort Firefly and Acorn Trail collections in this quilt. The quilt allows whoever cuddles under it to spend a moment with each print. These big round blocks are rather forgiving to piece and are a good choice for your first reverse appliqué.

Photo by Rossie Hutchinson

ROSSIE HUTCHINSON

Rossie Hutchinson is an award-winning modern quilter and international quilt teacher. Perhaps best known for founding the Flickr group Fresh Modern Quilts in 2008 and moderating it ever since, she also writes a popular quilting blog and regularly contributes her quilt patterns to books and magazines. Her quilts have appeared in *American Quilter*, *Quilting with a Modern Slant*, *Best Modern Quilts*, *101 Patchwork Projects*, and *Modern Quilts Unlimited*. Rossie lives in Michigan with her husband, dogs, and enormous library of crafts books. You can learn more about her by visiting her blog, r0ssie.blogspot.com. (Yes, that's a zero instead of an "o" in the blog address.)

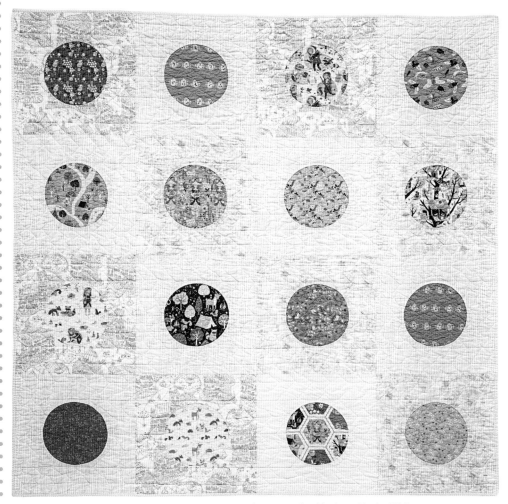

Moments, 80″ × 80″, designed and made by Rossie Hutchinson, quilted by Lynn Harris, 2014

MATERIALS

- **Black-and-white prints:** enough to make 16 squares 22″ × 22″ for block backgrounds*

- **White solid or muslin:** 5 yards* for facing fabric for blocks

- **Colorful print fabrics:** 1 fat quarter each of 16 different prints (If you intend to fussy cut, you may want to buy a larger piece.)

- **Backing:** 7½ yards

- **Binding:** ¾ yard

- **Batting:** 88″ × 88″

- **Removable fabric marker**

- **Round dinner plate:** approximately 10½″ in diameter, for use as a template

*If the fabrics have a 44″ usable width, ⅔ yard will yield 2 squares, and 5 yards each will be enough for the blocks and the reverse appliqué backing. If not, you will need 10 yards total of the black-and-white prints and 10 yards total for the reverse appliqué facings.

Cutting

From the black-and-white prints:

- Cut 16 squares 22″ × 22″.

From the white facing fabric:

- Cut 16 squares 22″ × 22″.

Preparing the Reverse Appliqués

1 Mark the center of each facing square by folding it in half lengthwise and widthwise and pressing along the folds to crease.

2 Use 2 pieces of tape to mark the circle template or plate into 4 equal quarters as shown.

3 Pair up a black-and-white print square and a facing square, right sides together, with the facing on top. Place the circle template or plate

on top of the squares, centering the tape marks on the creases. Use a removable fabric marker to draw around the shape to mark a circle on the facing square.

4 Pin the squares together on either side of the line, leaving room to sew on the line.

5 Using a slightly smaller stitch length than normal, machine stitch on the line, overlapping by a few stitches at the beginning and end of the circle.

6 Cut out the *center* of the circle about ½″ from the stitched line. Use scissors to clip the seam allow-ance on the inside of the circle to within a thread

Clip.

or 2 of the stitched circle so that the curved seam will sit flat.

TIP You can remove the center of the circle using scissors or a rotary cutter. Take care to maintain a ½″ seam allowance inside the stitched line.

7 Press to set the seam. Turn the block right side out by turning the edges of the facing through the hole. Line up the edges and use your hands to

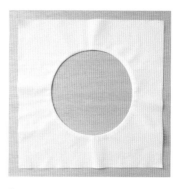

smooth out the block. Once it lies flat, press again.

8 Repeat Steps 3–7 with the remaining black-and-white print and backing squares to make 16 reverse-appliqué squares.

Reverse Appliquéing the Blocks

1 Place a colorful print fat quarter right side up on your work surface. Position a reverse-appliqué square right side up over the fat quarter so that

the part of the print you want to feature shows through the opening. Make sure that the bottom fabric extends at least ½˝ past each side of the opening.

2 Referring to Basting Appliqués (page 15), glue baste the fat quarter in place with small beads of glue ⅛˝ from the edge of the circle. Alternatively, you can pin it in place or use masking tape to secure it temporarily.

3 Topstitch around the circle ¼˝ from the edge through all 3 layers. Start and end in the same spot. Pull all the threads to the back of the block and knot them to secure. Press.

4 Use a rotary cutter to trim the block to 20½˝ × 20½˝ with the circle in the center. On the wrong side of the block, carefully trim the fat quarter away, leaving a ¼˝ seam allowance. Do *not* trim the backing fabric.

5 Repeat Steps 1–4 to make a total of 16 blocks.

Assembling the Quilt

Use a ¼˝ seam allowance. Press after each seam.

Arrange the blocks in a 4 × 4 grid. When you are satisfied with the layout, join the blocks into rows and then join the rows.

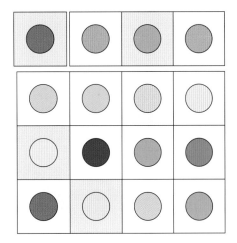

Finishing

1 Refer to Finishing a Quilt (page 150) to layer, baste, and quilt as desired.

2 Refer to Binding (page 151) or use your preferred method to make and attach the binding.

3 If you plan to hang the quilt, refer to Hanging Sleeves (page 154) to add a sleeve.

Rossie's Tip

When sewing the edge of a large circle, it is more important to keep the curve smooth than to stay exactly on the line. If you find that your stitching has wandered off a little bit, bring it back to the line gradually rather than making a quick adjustment that will show the error.

Photo by Lindsay Wilkinson Photography, LLC

Alison Glass Author of the popular book *Alison Glass Appliqué*, designer Alison Glass is enthusiastic about the many design possibilities made available by appliqué. Coming from a home decor background, Alison tends to begin with an idea for a project that she would like to have in her home; she then figures out the construction methods to make that project a reality and frequently turns to various appliqué techniques.

Appliqué allows her to incorporate organic forms into her quilts and other projects. She appreciates the organic nature of the appliqué process.

"I like that it is more along the lines of drawing with fabric.... You can let the project develop as you go," she says. This organic style is particularly notable in Alison's quilt *Overgrown*, which took home the viewers' choice prize at the inaugural QuiltCon in 2013. Like many of her appliqué projects, *Overgrown* features large-scale appliqué, which Alison enjoys because it moves the focus to the entire composition of the quilt rather than the individual blocks.

You can learn more about Alison and her work at alisonglass.com.

Overgrown, 76˝ × 84˝, designed and made by Alison Glass, quilted by Lisa Sipes, 2012
Photo courtesy of Lucky Spool Media, LLC

Field Day (detail), 36″ × 96″, designed and quilted by Alison Glass, 2014
Photo by Nicole Daksiewicz

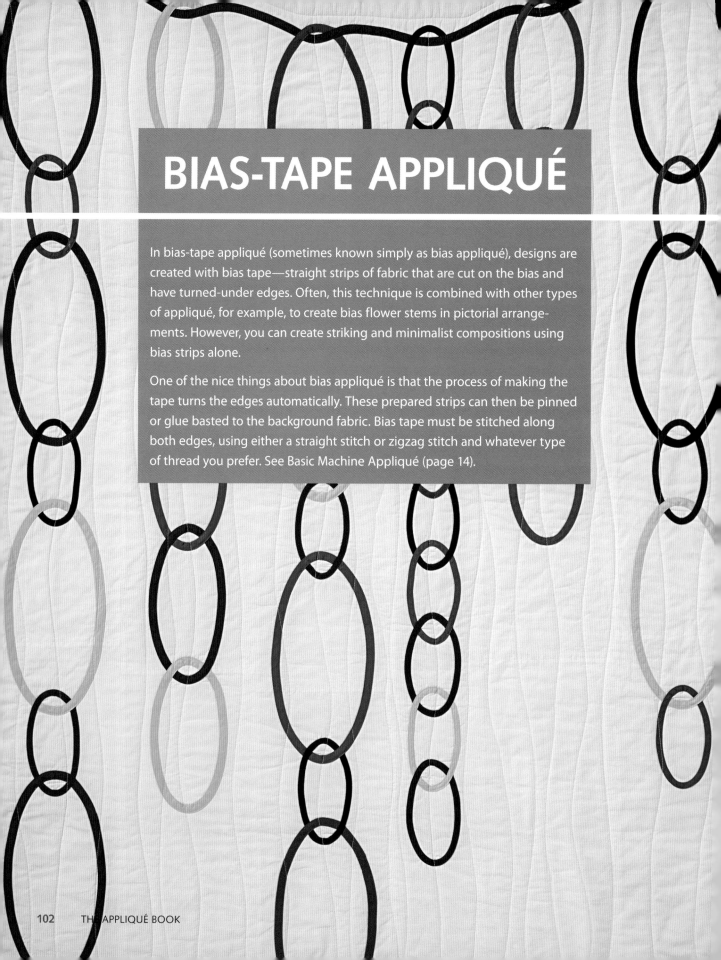

BIAS-TAPE APPLIQUÉ

In bias-tape appliqué (sometimes known simply as bias appliqué), designs are created with bias tape—straight strips of fabric that are cut on the bias and have turned-under edges. Often, this technique is combined with other types of appliqué, for example, to create bias flower stems in pictorial arrangements. However, you can create striking and minimalist compositions using bias strips alone.

One of the nice things about bias appliqué is that the process of making the tape turns the edges automatically. These prepared strips can then be pinned or glue basted to the background fabric. Bias tape must be stitched along both edges, using either a straight stitch or zigzag stitch and whatever type of thread you prefer. See Basic Machine Appliqué (page 14).

Making Bias Tape

Bias-tape makers make quick work of creating the long bias strips necessary for bias appliqué. Read the instructions for the bias-tape maker to learn how wide to cut the fabric strips.

1 Following the instructions for the bias-tape maker, cut a series of bias strips in the appropriate width. The stretch and give in the bias grain allows the bias tape to trace smooth curves.

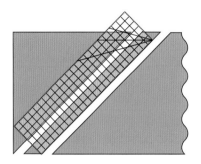

2 Stitch the strips together end to end with diagonal seams. Press the seam allowances open.

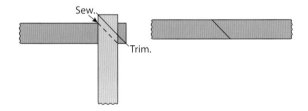

3 Feed an end of the strip into the wide end of the bias-tape maker. Use a pin to advance the strip through the maker, which will fold the edges together as they come out the other end.

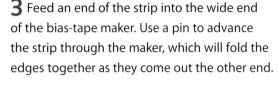

4 Use an iron and steam if necessary to press the tape flat as it emerges from the narrow end of the bias-tape maker.

5 Pull the bias-tape maker along the length of the strip an inch or 2 at a time, sliding the iron directly behind it to press the emerging tape. Take care when you reach seams in the tape.

Training Bias Tape to a Curve

It can sometimes be helpful to use steam to train bias tape to take the particular curves you want to create. To do this, press the tape with a steam iron using one hand, and use the other hand to gently manipulate the tape into the shape that you desire. Once the tape cools, it will hold the curve by itself.

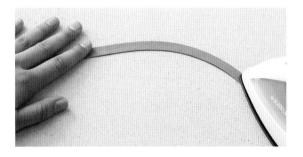

PAPER CHAINS

by Debbie Grifka

THIS PROJECT FEATURES:

- Bias-tape appliqué
- Machine stitching
- Freezer-paper templates for marking placement
- Pin basting

Bias-tape appliqué was one of the first classes I took after learning to quilt. I made several small quilts using Celtic designs and enjoyed it so much that I thought, "What else can I do with this technique?"

The answer is to draw with fabric. Since then, I've done all kinds of designs with bias appliqué, from abstract pictures to circles to energetic squiggly lines.

Celtic appliqué traditionally includes weaving the bias strips over and under each other. Ends are hidden underneath an "over" spot. *Paper Chains* continues this tradition so that no raw edges are visible.

Photo by Heather Grifka

DEBBIE GRIFKA

Debbie Grifka will never forget the excitement she felt on finding the *Modern Quilt Workshop* by Weeks Ringle and Bill Kerr in 2006. She knew right away that she wanted to make quilts with the same kind of feeling, and her journey to her own style jumped forward.

Further inspired by the work of Gwen Marston, Jacquie Gering, and others in the online modern quilting community, Debbie now describes her style as graphic, modern minimalism. She focuses on making quilts with clean lines and bold shapes, whether the colors are deep and intense or low-contrast neutrals and whether the technique is piecing or appliqué.

Debbie's work has been displayed at both Paducah and Houston and featured in various magazines and books. She focuses on her pattern business, Esch House Quilts, and sharing her love of modern quilting and appliqué through teaching.

Debbie blogs at eschhousequilts.com and is active on several social media sites. She is vice president of the Ann Arbor, Michigan, Modern Quilt Guild and a member of the Greater Ann Arbor Quilt Guild.

MATERIALS

Unless otherwise noted, all measurements refer to 40˝-wide 100% cotton quilting fabric.

- **Assorted solid fabrics:** 1 fat quarter each of red, orange, yellow, green, and purple for chain appliqués

- **Blue solid fabric:** 1 yard for chain appliqués and binding

- **White solid fabric:** 2¾ yards for background

- **Batting:** 54˝ × 74˝

- **Backing:** 3¼ yards

- **Thread:** to match appliqué fabrics

- **Removable fabric marker**

- **⅜˝ bias-tape maker**

- **½˝ bias-tape maker**

- **Freezer paper:** 18˝ wide, 1 yard

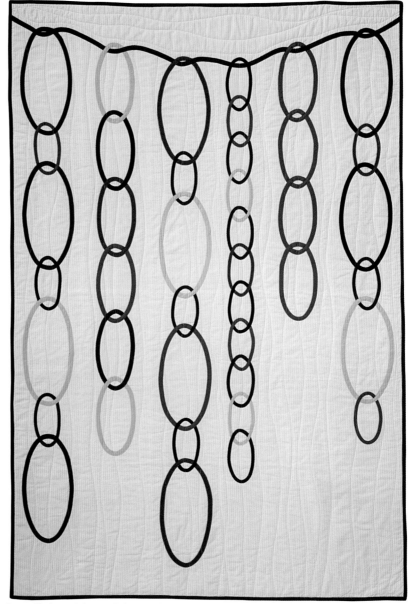

Paper Chains, 45¾˝ × 65½˝, designed, made, and quilted by Debbie Grifka, 2014

Cutting

NOTE: The 1˝ strips will make ½˝ bias tape for the large and medium links and top strip. The ¾˝ strips will make ⅜˝ bias tape for the small links. Check the width recommended by your bias-tape maker instructions and adjust the cut width of the strip size if necessary.

From the white fabric:

- Cut 9 strips 8½˝ × width of fabric for the background.

- Cut 2 strips 5¾˝ × width of fabric for the background.

From the blue fabric:

- Cut 1 strip 18˝ × width of fabric.

  Subcut *on the bias* 8 strips 1˝ wide and 2 strips ¾˝ wide.

  Set aside the remaining fabric for 2½˝-wide straight-grain binding.

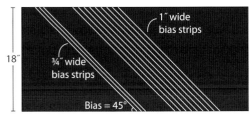

To make long strips, cut bias strips across the widest part of the fabric.

From the red fabric:

- Cut *on the bias* 2 strips 1˝ wide and 4 strips ¾˝ wide.

From the orange fabric:

- Cut *on the bias* 4 strips 1˝ wide and 2 strips ¾˝ wide.

From the yellow fabric:

- Cut *on the bias* 6 strips 1˝ wide and 2 strips ¾˝ wide.

From the green fabric:

- Cut *on the bias* 6 strips 1˝ wide and 3 strips ¾˝ wide.

From the purple fabric:

- Cut *on the bias* 3 strips 1˝ wide and 3 strips ¾˝ wide.

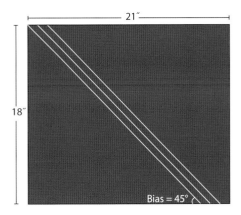

Preparing the Bias Strips

Refer to Bias-Tape Appliqué (page 102) for information about techniques. All seams are ¼˝. Press all seams open.

1 Matching colors and strip widths, sew the bias strips together end to end with diagonal seams.

2 Using bias-tape makers, make the 1˝ strips into ½˝ bias tape and the ¾˝ strips into ⅜˝ bias tape.

Preparing the Background Fabric

1 Sew the white 8½″-wide strips together along the short ends and subcut 5 strips 65½″ in length. Fold each piece in half widthwise and press to mark the center of the strip.

2 Sew the white 5¾″-wide strips together end to end and subcut 1 strip 65½″ in length. Fold in half widthwise and press to mark the center of the strip.

3 Referring to the *Paper Chains* patterns (pullout page P2), trace and cut out 4 large, 4 medium, and 7 small oval patterns onto the dull side of the freezer paper, making sure to include all the markings. Each freezer-paper template can be used at least 3 times.

NOTE: Trace each oval separately. The patterns are nested only to conserve space.

4 To mark appliqué placement lines on column 1, use a dry iron to press 4 large and 3 small oval

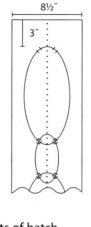

freezer-paper templates onto an 8½″ × 65½″ white strip, aligning the centerline of each oval with the crease you pressed in the center of the strip. Begin 3″ from the top raw edge and overlap the ends at the double lines. Using a removable fabric marker, trace around the templates, peeling back the freezer paper to complete the tracing where the templates overlap. Include the 4 sets of hatch marks as you trace because they mark the points where you start and stop stitching. After tracing, peel away the freezer-paper templates.

5 Following the appliqué placement diagram (page 109), fuse and trace the templates to the remaining columns of background fabric in the same manner as in Step 4. Refer to the diagram to see how far from the upper edge of the column each series of links should begin.

Applying the Bias Strips

Stitching the First Link in a Column

1 Start by positioning the raw edge of the bias tape between the 2 top right marks on the link. Pin in place around the traced ring, centering the tape over the traced line and clipping the tape so that the second raw edge meets the first between the upper right pair of hatch marks.

Pin, starting here.

2 Referring to the stitching guide (page 109), use matching thread and a straight machine stitch to sew around the inside edge of the link in a counterclockwise direction, stitching close to the folded edge of the bias tape. Start at the upper right hatch marks.

Stop stitching at the first upper left hatch mark, backstitching or leaving a long thread tail to tie off. Begin stitching again at the second upper left mark. This will leave an open space through

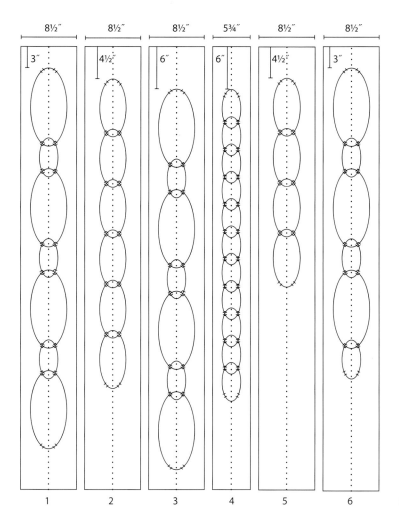

8½″	8½″	8½″	5¾″	8½″	8½″
3″	4½″	6″	6″	4½″	3″
1	2	3	4	5	6

Appliqué placement

which you can weave the final piece of bias tape, linking all the chains together along the top of the quilt.

3 Continue stitching through the lower left hatch marks. Stop stitching at the first lower right hatch mark, backstitching or leaving a thread tail to tie off; begin stitching again at the second lower right mark. This will leave an opening into which you can tuck the raw edges of the next link.

4 Stop stitching the bias strip when you reach the upper right pair of hatch marks again.

5 Stitch along the outer edge of the chain, stopping and starting in the same places as on the inner edge. The top link of each column *must* follow this same pattern.

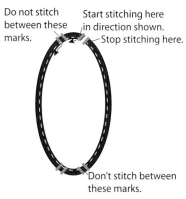

Do not stitch between these marks.

Start stitching here in direction shown.

Stop stitching here.

Don't stitch between these marks.

Stitching guide

Stitching the Remaining Links

1 Referring to the quilt assembly diagram for placement, repeat Stitching the First Link in a Column, Steps 1–4 (page 108), but do *not* leave the upper left hatch marks open on the lower links. Continue stitching the links in each column, stopping and starting the bias tape between the upper right marks and tucking the raw edges of the tape beneath the opening in the previous chain.

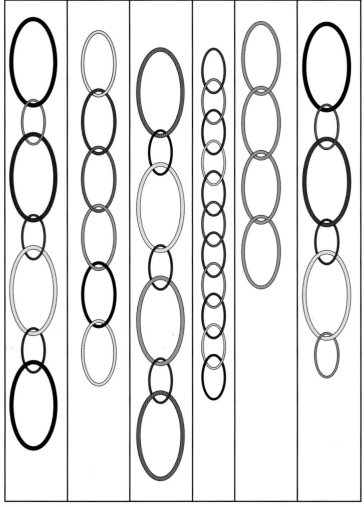

Quilt assembly

It is also possible to add and sew all the links of a particular color at one time. In this case, you must stop and start stitching at *every* intersection to leave room for the previous and next links to be placed **TIP** and sewn properly.

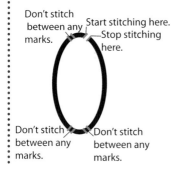

Don't stitch between any marks.

Start stitching here.
Stop stitching here.

Don't stitch between any marks.

Don't stitch between any marks.

2 After you have placed and stitched each link in the chains, go back and use matching thread to stitch all the openings closed, except in the top of the first link in each column. This will also secure the raw edges of the bias tape that have been tucked beneath them.

Leave the top left opening in the first link in each column open so you can weave the top ribbon through after you have assembled the quilt.

Leave open only on 1st link in a column.

Stitch top link down.

Assembling the Quilt and Appliquéing the Ribbon

1 Referring to the quilt assembly diagram (page 110), sew the columns together.

2 Starting about 1½˝ from the upper left edge, weave the ½˝ blue bias strip under the left side and over the right side of the top of each top link to connect them all. Be sure to cover the top right raw edges of each link. Stitch the strip in place along both edges, stopping and starting where the blue tape passes under another color.

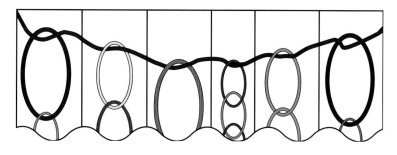

3 Using matching thread, stitch the rest of the openings closed.

Finishing

1 Refer to Finishing a Quilt (page 150) to layer, baste, and quilt as desired.

2 Refer to Binding (page 151) or use your preferred method to make and attach the binding.

3 If you plan to hang the quilt, refer to Hanging Sleeves (page 154) to add a sleeve.

Debbie's Bias-Tape Appliqué Tips

To get the best results when using a bias-tape maker, keep the tip of your iron just touching the tape maker as you pull the bias strips through it.

When tucking the raw edges of a bias strip under another bias strip, trim the ends on an angle that matches the curve of the top strip.

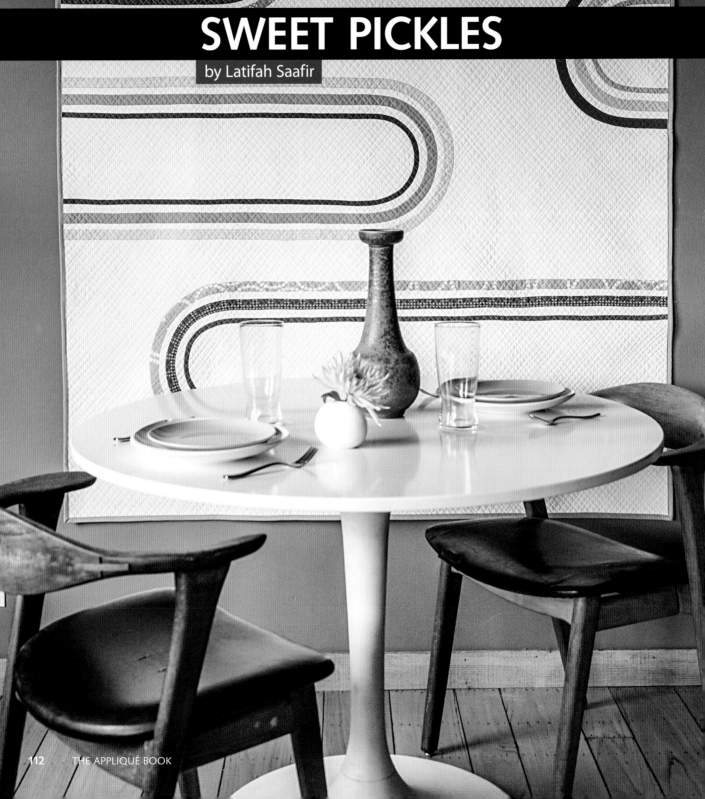

SWEET PICKLES

by Latifah Saafir

Finished quilt size: 60″ × 70″

THIS PROJECT FEATURES:

- Turned-edge appliqué
- Bias-tape appliqué
- Machine stitching

Bias-tape appliqué is traditionally sewn at least partially by hand and is featured either in Celtic quilts or as vines and stems. *Sweet Pickles* shows how you can use bias-tape appliqué to create bold, modern designs, and it simplifies the process by topstitching the bias tape by machine.

LATIFAH SAAFIR

Photo by Latifah Saafir

Latifah Saafir is known for her bold and innovative modern quilts. Combining her training as an engineer with her lifelong passion for sewing, Latifah creates designs that are graphic and contemporary, featuring challenging techniques with meticulous attention to detail. A co-founder of both the Los Angeles Modern Quilt Guild and the worldwide Modern Quilt Guild, Latifah teaches workshops to guilds around the country and has a line of patterns available at latifahsaafirstudios.com.

MATERIALS

- **White solid:** 4 yards for background *OR* 2 yards 90″+

- **Appliqué fabrics:** ½ yard each of 15 different fabrics for bias tape (You will have some leftover fabric, but this size reduces the number of cuts you will need to seam together for the long strips.)

- **Batting:** 68″ × 78″

- **Backing:** 4 yards

- **Binding:** ¾ yard

- **Thread to match appliqué fabrics**

- **Removable fabric marker that does not disappear with heat**

- **1″ bias-tape maker**

- **½″ bias-tape maker**

- **Freezer paper or template plastic** *(optional)*

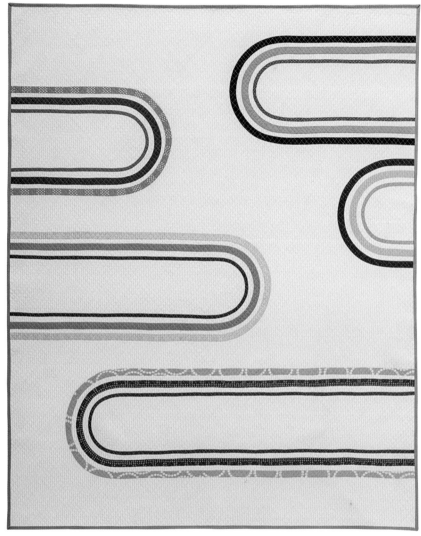

Sweet Pickles, 60″ × 70″, designed, made, and quilted by Latifah Saafir, 2014

Cutting

From the white background fabric:

- Cut or piece a rectangle measuring 60″ × 70″.

From the appliqué fabrics:

- Referring to the quilt assembly diagram at right, choose 3 appliqué fabrics for each shape—A, B, C, D, and E.

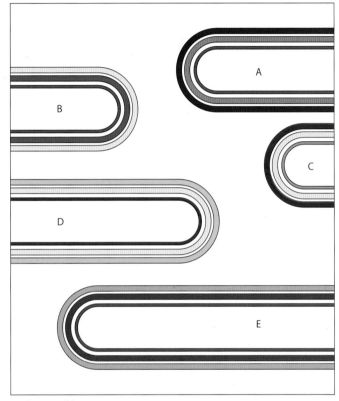

Quilt assembly

NOTE: *The 2″ strips are for 1″ bias tape and the 1″ strips are for ½″ bias tape. Check the width recommended in the instructions for your bias-tape maker and adjust the strip size if necessary.*

Shape A:

- From each of 2 fabrics, cut *on the bias* 4 strips (8 total) 2″ wide.

- From the third fabric, cut *on the bias* 4 strips 1″ wide.

Shape B:

- From each of 2 fabrics, cut *on the bias* 3 strips (6 total) 2″ wide.

- From the third fabric, cut *on the bias* 3 strips 1″ wide.

Shape C:

- From each of 2 fabrics, cut *on the bias* 3 strips (6 total) 2″ wide.

- From the third fabric, cut *on the bias* 3 strips 1″ wide.

Shape D:

- From each of 2 fabrics, cut *on the bias* 5 strips (10 total) 2″ wide.

- From the third fabric, cut *on the bias* 5 strips 1″ wide.

Shape E:

- From each of 2 fabrics, cut *on the bias* 6 strips (12 total) 2″ wide.

- From the third fabric, cut *on the bias* 6 strips 1″ wide.

Preparing the Bias Strips

Refer to Making Bias Tape (page 103) for techniques.

1 Matching colors and strip widths, sew the bias strips together end to end with diagonal seams. Press.

2 Using the bias-tape makers and an iron, make the 2″ strips into 1″ bias tape and the 1″ strips into ½″ bias tape.

Preparing the Background Fabric

1 Referring to the *Sweet Pickles* patterns (pullout page P2), trace and cut out 1 copy each of Pattern A and 3 copies of Pattern B. For the B templates, cut 1 on each of the 3 lines. You can use paper, freezer paper, or template plastic.

2 As shown in the marking diagram (below right), use a fabric marker to place marks close to the edge of the fabric 12″ and 32″ from the top left corner of the background fabric. From the top right corner, mark down 5″, 22″, and 51″.

3 Mark the appliqué shapes, starting with Shape B. Align a long edge of Template A at the 12″ mark on the left side of the raw edge of the quilt. Trace the 3 short lines at each end of Template A.

4 Extend the lines from Template A 16″ into the background fabric.

5 Align each copy of Template B with the lines you traced in Step 4. Transfer the curved lines to the background fabric.

6 In the same manner, mark Shapes A, C, D, and E:

- **Shape A:** Start 5″ from the upper right corner; extend the Template A lines 22″.

- **Shape C:** Start 22″ from the upper right corner; extend the Template A lines 6″.

- **Shape D:** Start 32″ from the upper left corner; extend the Template A lines 31″.

- **Shape E:** Start 51″ from the upper right corner; extend the Template A lines 44″.

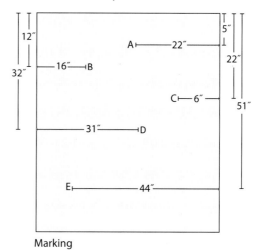

Marking

Applying the Bias Strips

1 Center a 1″ bias strip along an outer marked guideline. Using thread that matches the bias tape, begin stitching very close to the inside edge with a straight stitch. Guide the fabric around the curve as you sew, taking care not to stretch the bias tape. Continue to the edge of the background fabric. If the bias strip extends past the edge of the background, do not trim it until you have stitched both edges.

2 Using a steam iron and high heat, press the stitched bias tape slowly to relax it into place.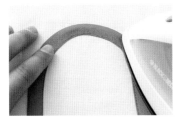

3 Stitch the outer edge of the bias tape, making sure the tape lies flat. Press again using steam and high heat.

4 Trim the ends of the bias strip even with the edge of the background fabric.

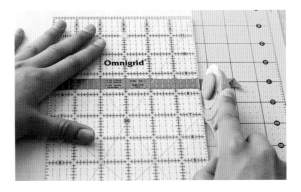

5 Refer to Steps 1–4 to stitch a 1″-wide bias-tape strip on the centerline of the shape and a ½″-wide bias-tape strip on the inside line.

6 Repeat Steps 1–5 for each shape.

Finishing

1 Refer to Finishing a Quilt (page 150) to layer, baste, and quilt as desired.

2 Refer to Binding (page 151) or use your preferred method to make and attach the binding.

3 If you plan to hang the quilt, refer to Hanging Sleeves (page 154) to add a sleeve.

Latifah's Bias-Tape Appliqué Tips

You can use your standard open-toe foot to sew the bias tape, but an edge-guide foot or zipper foot makes it easier.

Sew slowly when sewing bias tape appliqué, especially around the curves.

If you accidentally sew off the bias tape and onto the background fabric, stop sewing and cut your thread. Use a seam ripper to remove the stitches that went awry. Stitch over the last few stitches and then continue sewing.

Be careful not to stretch the bias tape as you sew the inside edge!

Photo by Caroline Valites

Denyse Schmidt

Considered by some to be a founding member of the modern quilting movement, Denyse Schmidt began making appliqué quilts early on.

"I explored a lot of different hand-appliqué methods, and I liked needle-turn the best because it has a soft edge … and you can do very nice curves with needle-turn," she says.

Denyse's appliqué quilt designs have a hand-drawn immediacy to them. Although she sometimes uses templates, she also sometimes simply draws shapes directly onto fabric or cuts them freehand.

"I think that people are often intimidated by appliqué because we are always intimidated by things that we don't understand … but once you identify the technique that suits your style, or if you know about different techniques and find out that it's not as hard as you think, that is totally freeing."

She has released some stand-alone appliqué patterns and includes even more in her most recent book, *Denyse Schmidt: Modern Quilts, Traditional Inspiration*. To see more of Denyse's appliqué work, visit her website, dsquilts.com.

Flowering Vine, 80˝ × 88˝, designed, made, and quilted by Denyse Schmidt, 2012
Photo by Denyse Schmidt

Hills and Hollers, 66″ × 88″, designed, made, and quilted by Denyse Schmidt, 2009
Photo by Denyse Schmidt

FREE-FORM APPLIQUÉ

I use the term "free-form appliqué" to encompass techniques that feature improvisational elements. Some of these techniques, such as Broderie Perse, use the fabric print as a guide for cutting appliqués, while others embrace a completely freehand technique for cutting.

Despite these differences, all these techniques share an improvisational approach to arranging the appliqués on the background fabric. Sometimes guidelines are used to help with placement, but generally the appliqués are arranged without reference to a placement diagram. As with reverse appliqué and bias-tape appliqué, you can use many different basic techniques for free-form appliqué.

In the projects that follow, you will learn about several different approaches to free-form appliqué. Each project features different construction techniques that will build upon the skills you've learned from the previous chapters.

The beauty of free-form appliqué, however, is the freedom that it gives you to experiment and try out new ideas. I hope these projects will provide guidelines, construction ideas, and inspiration for your own explorations into free-form approaches to appliqué.

CORONA DE FLORES
by Casey York

Finished size: 65″ × 55″

THIS PROJECT FEATURES:

- Broderie Perse
- Raw-edge appliqué
- Fusible appliqué
- Machine stitching

Broderie Perse, meaning "Persian embroidery," was originally used as a way of stretching precious and expensive pieces of chintz fabric. Individual motifs were cut from the printed fabric, arranged into inventive compositions, and appliquéd to a plain background cloth.

Broderie Perse is a great technique for using some of the wonderful large-scale prints that are on the market today.

In this project, flowers inspired by Mexican folk art are arranged into a lush wreath on a white background. This is just one possible arrangement, however, and the techniques that follow can be used to create whatever type of composition inspires you. I used a raw-edge appliqué technique, but you could easily needle-turn the Broderie Perse appliqués by hand if you wish.

Photo by Randall Kahn

CASEY YORK

Casey York is a quilt designer and author known for her bold, minimalist appliqué quilts. For more information about Casey, see About the Author (page 159).

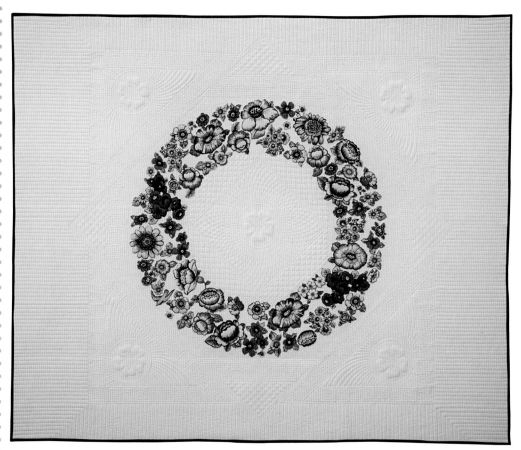

Corona de Flores, 65″ × 55″, designed and made by Casey York, quilted by Ann McNew, 2014

MATERIALS

Unless otherwise noted, all measurements refer to 40″-wide 100% cotton quilting fabric.

- **White:** 3¼ yards for pieced background *OR* 1¾ yards if fabric is 90″+ wide

- **Appliqué fabric:** 1–2 yards of large-scale floral print (Yardage will vary depending on print.)

- **Backing:** 3⅝ yards

- **Batting:** 73″ × 63″

- **Binding:** ⅞ yard for bias binding *OR* ⅔ yard for straight-grain binding

- **Double-sided lightweight fusible web:** 15″ wide, 3 yards per yard of appliqué fabric

- **Invisible thread:** for machine appliqué, if desired

- **Removable fabric marker**

TIP

The appliqué shapes used in this technique depend on the motifs in the fabric you choose. Generally, fabric designs with minimal overlapping and some space between motifs work best. It also helps if there is a single-color background behind the motifs that will blend with your base background.

The number of motifs that you can cut from a yard of fabric will vary depending on the print. Try to buy enough yardage so that you can cut out 60 or more motifs of various sizes for a full-looking arrangement.

Cutting

From the white background fabric: Cut or piece 1 rectangle 55″ × 65″.

Preparing the Appliqués

1 Prepare the appliqué fabric for cutting out motifs. If the motifs you wish to cut out are closely spaced, fuse lengths of fusible web to the *wrong* side of the fabric to cover the entire length of fabric, following the manufacturer's directions. Because there is little space between the various motifs, this will not result in a significant waste of fabric or fusible web.

2 If the motifs you wish to cut out are widely spaced, you can cut out smaller pieces of fusible web and place them over the motifs you wish to cut out. The fusible web is translucent, and you will be able to see the print of the fabric through it to enable correct placement. The fusible web pieces should extend about ¼″ past the edges of the motifs that you wish to cut out.

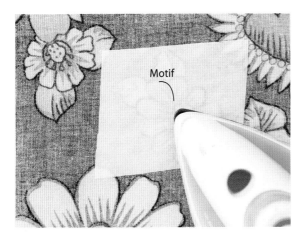

Motif

3 With the right side of the fabric facing up, cut out the motifs you wish to use. If you wish to create a densely packed appliqué arrangement, as in the model, try to cut out motifs in a wide variety of sizes. Large-scale motifs will anchor your arrangement, and small-scale ones are useful for filling in gaps.

TIP If the background color of the appliqué fabrics contrasts with the color of the quilt background, you will want to cut very close to the outlines of each motif. If the background color of the appliqué fabrics matches that of the quilt background, you can cut more loosely around the appliqués because they will blend into the background. If you don't need to cut out the tiny details of the motifs, it will be easier to stitch around the appliqués.

Assembling the Quilt Top

1 Mark the wreath shape that you will fill in with appliqués. Find the center of the background fabric by folding it in half lengthwise and width-wise and pressing to create creases; the center is the point where the 2 creases meet.

2 Using a tape measure or ruler and a removable fabric marker, make a series of marks 10˝ from the

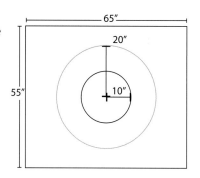

center point of the background fabric. Make another series of marks 20˝ from the center point. These 2 sets of markings will form the inner and outer edges of a ring, within which you will place your appliqués.

3 Arrange the appliqués within the ring, removing the paper backing from the fusible web as you go. When you are satisfied with

the placement, pin each appliqué in place with a single pin. Depending on the type of fabric marker used, you may need to remove the markings on the quilt top before fusing so as not to make permanent marks.

TIP Start with the largest appliqués and distribute them evenly around the ring. Next, place the medium-sized appliqués among the large-scale ones. Fill in any small gaps with small-scale appliqués to create a densely packed arrangement.

4 Referring to the fusible manufacturer's directions, use an iron to fuse the appliqués permanently into place. Remove the pins before you press each appliqué. You can press portions of multiple appliqués at once; there is no need to try to press each appliqué individually.

5 Using invisible thread and a zigzag or blanket stitch, machine stitch around the edge of each appliqué to secure it to the background fabric.

Finishing

1 Refer to Finishing a Quilt (page 150) to layer, baste, and quilt as desired.

2 Refer to Binding (page 151) or use your preferred method to make and attach the binding.

3 If you plan to hang the quilt, refer to Hanging Sleeves (page 154) to add a sleeve.

Casey's Appliqué Tips

Because the arrangement of the appliqués in Broderie Perse depends on the motifs that are being appliquéd, and because the number of motifs per yard of fabric varies with the print, I like to buy extra fabric for this type of project (or be certain that I can get more if I need it).

It also helps to embrace the free-form nature of this type of project, letting the fabric you have available determine the final arrangement of the appliqués on the quilt. For example, make a smaller or sparser arrangement if you are working with fewer appliqués, or enlarge your arrangement if you have a large number of appliqués to work with.

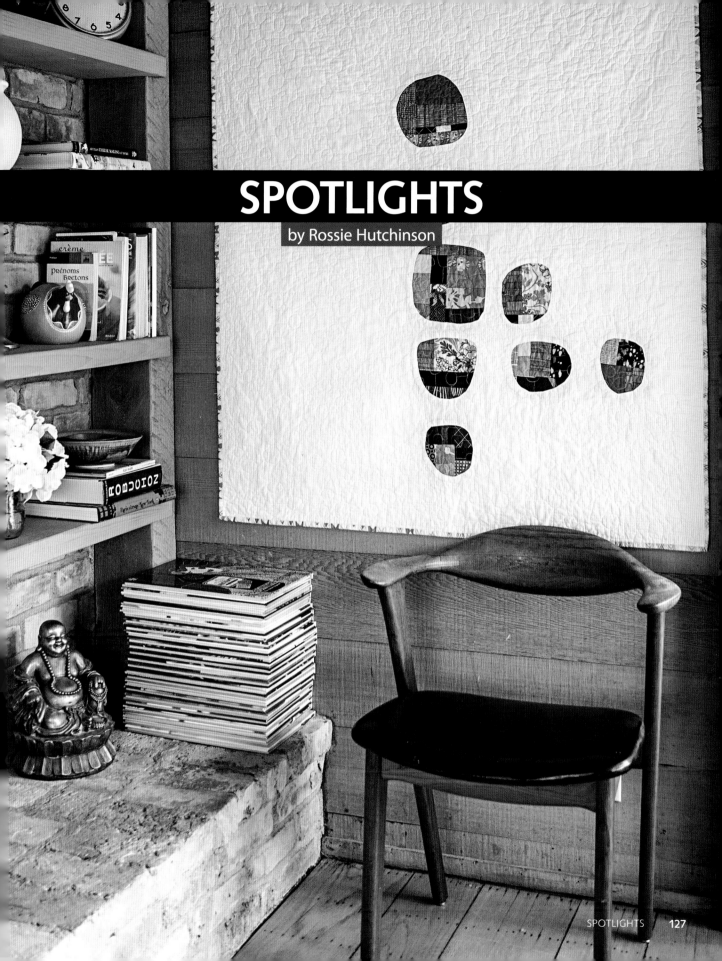

SPOTLIGHTS
by Rossie Hutchinson

Spotlights by Rossie Hutchinson

Finished quilt size:
40˝ × 45˝
Finished improv block size:
roughly 6˝ × 6˝

THIS PROJECT FEATURES:

• Improvisation

• Reverse appliqué

• Stitch-and-turn appliqué

• Machine stitching

• Glue basting

Sometimes the beauty of improvisational scrap piecing is lost in the craziness of a crowded quilt top. Here, I'm using reverse appliqué to isolate and highlight special pieces of patchwork. The spotlights are improvisationally shaped, making a beautiful and cohesive top.

Photo by Rossie Hutchinson

ROSSIE HUTCHINSON

Rossie Hutchinson is an award-winning modern quilter and international quilt teacher. For more information about Rossie, see her profile in *Moments* (page 96).

Spotlights, 40˝ × 45˝, designed, made, and quilted by Rossie Hutchinson, 2014

MATERIALS

Unless otherwise noted, all measurements refer to 40˝-wide 100% cotton quilting fabric.

- **White solid:** 1½ yards for background

- **White solid:** ½ yard for appliqué facings

- **Blue and teal scraps in varied sizes, from at least 10 different fabrics:** to total roughly 1 yard for improvisational piecing

- **Backing:** 3 yards

- **Batting:** 48˝ × 53˝

- **Binding:** ½ yard

- **Removable fabric marker**

Making the Improv Blocks

Use a ¼˝ seam allowance and press after each addition.

1 Begin by sewing 2 scraps together. Continue to add pieces without making any value-based assessments of your work. Use a simple production mode in which you combine small pieces of fabric into larger pieces quickly, without taking too long to make decisions or think about the outcome. Just make the units bigger and bigger without worrying what they look like.

NOTE: *Having trouble with Step 1? See Rossie's Improv Piecing Tips (page 131).*

2 When you have a few blocks, stop and look at them. Decide if you want to keep making blocks in the same way or make some adjustments. Perhaps you will decide to add colors to the mix, or subtract colors. Feel free to reject some of your blocks or cut them up and edit them.

3 When you start making blocks again, follow the simple production mode described in Step 1 until you have made 8 improvisational blocks about 6˝ × 6˝ or a little larger. You don't need to square up the blocks, as the edges will be trimmed away later.

Preparing the Background

1 Trim the background fabric to 40″ × 45″. Press the background fabric and place it on your design wall with the *right* side facing you. Arrange the improv blocks on the background fabric until you find a pleasing arrangement.

> **TIP** Because the improv blocks will be removed from the background fabric before the final assembly, label the blocks or take a photo of the arrangement so that it is easy to remember which block belongs where.

2 Take an improv block off the design wall, mark its original position, and place the block on the facing fabric. Using the block as a guide, cut a piece of facing fabric that is about ½″ larger all around than the block.

3 Place the facing fabric wrong side up on top of the improv block. Use the fabric marker to draw a big blobby shape on the fabric over the block. Be sure to keep the edges of the shape at least ½″ from the edges of the improv block. For this project, aim to produce an organic shape, neither perfectly oval nor circular, but without sharp angles.

> **TIP** You can draw and redraw these lines; they don't show in the final work. If you are having a hard time being imperfect, try drawing the shape with your nondominant hand. For example, if you are right-handed, draw the shape with your left hand.

4 Set the improv block aside. Pin the marked facing, wrong side out, to the background fabric in the place of the improv block on your design wall.

5 Repeat Steps 2–4 with each block until you have a piece of background fabric with 8 pieces of facing fabric arranged on it.

6 Take the background fabric to the sewing machine. Sew on the marked line of each facing piece. Overlap the stitches at the beginning of each stitching line to secure.

7 Using scissors or a rotary cutter, cut out the *center* of each stitched shape, leaving a ½″ seam allowance. Clip the seam allowance within a thread or 2 of the stitched shape every ½″; make the clips closer together in areas where the shape makes tight turns.

Clip.

8 Press to set the seams and then turn each opening right side out by pulling the edges of the facing through the opening to the wrong side of the background. Flatten out the facings and press.

Stitching the Appliqué

1 Place an improv block right side up on your work surface. Center the corresponding opening in the background fabric over it, also right side up. Check that the improv block extends at least ½″ beyond all sides of the opening.

2 Glue baste the block in place with a small bead of glue ⅛″ from the edge of the opening. See Basting Appliqués (page 15). Alternatively, you can use pins or masking tape to secure it temporarily.

3 Using thread that matches the background fabric, top-stitch close to the edge of the opening to reverse appliqué the background to the block. Start and end in the same spot. Pull all the threads to the back of the block and knot them. Press.

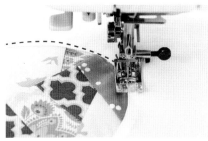

4 Use scissors to trim the extra facing fabric and improv block to within ½″ from the stitched seam. Be careful not to cut the background fabric.

5 Repeat Steps 1–4 to reverse appliqué the remaining blocks.

Finishing

1 Refer to Finishing a Quilt (page 150) to layer, baste, and quilt as desired.

2 Refer to Binding (page 151) or use your preferred method to make and attach the binding.

3 If you plan to hang the quilt, refer to Hanging Sleeves (page 154) to add a sleeve.

Rossie's Improv Piecing Tips

Having trouble in Step 1? Try one of the following books for a more in-depth set of instructions on cutting loose and piecing improvisationally:

- Sunday Morning Quilts *by Cheryl Arkison and Amanda Jean Nyberg (especially the section on sewing a slab of fabric)*

- Lucky Spool's Essential Guide to Modern Quiltmaking *(especially Denyse Schmidt's section on improvisational patchwork)*

- The Improv Handbook for Modern Quilters *by Sherri Lynn Wood*

- Quilt Improv *by Lucie Summers (especially the section on pieced squares)*

Photo by Jessica Downey

Bari J. Ackerman

Although her technique shares characteristics with Broderie Perse appliqué, Bari J. Ackerman prefers to think of it as collage. The concepts of free-form cutting and arranging are central to her work. Bari J. started making collages by stitching down appliqués around their perimeters but soon realized that she could use quilting to both secure her appliqués and add additional texture and interest to the fabrics. This continues to be one of her signature techniques.

Bari J. finds the process of appliqué freeing. "With the collage … putting together the composition is like putting together a painting … and to me that's really relaxing," she says.

She begins by cutting out a variety of motifs and then arranges them one at a time on a base material, building the composition as she goes. As described in her 2011 book *Inspired to Sew by Bari J.*, she then free-motion quilts over the entire composition to secure the appliqués.

Bari continues to use her appliqué collages to embellish all types of objects, including clothing. She wants the finished work to look fashionable and subtle rather than eccentric, and she attempts to make her appliquéd addition "look like it was built into the piece … to begin with."

You can learn more about Bari and view more of her work at her website, barijdesigns.com.

Flowering Container Garden Pillow, designed and made by Bari J. Ackerman, 2010

Garden Tunic, designed and made by Bari J. Ackerman, 2010

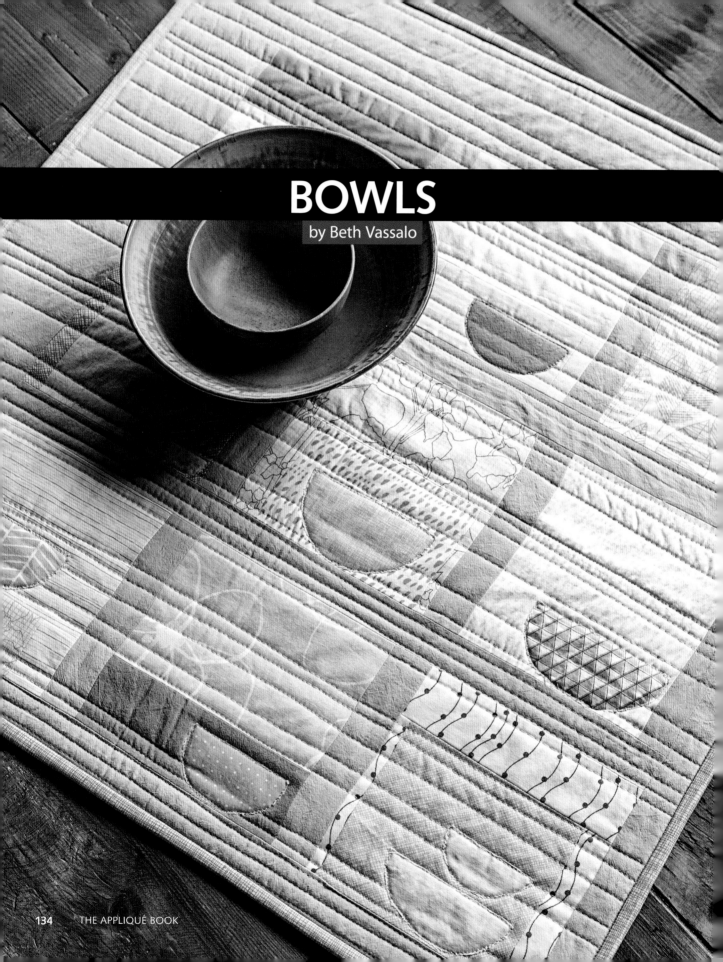

BOWLS

by Beth Vassalo

Finished quilt size: 23″ × 23″ • Finished block size: 5½″ × 5½″

THIS PROJECT FEATURES:

- Piecing
- Freehand cutting
- Improv arrangement
- Machine stitching
- Raw-edge appliqué

I really enjoy using appliqué techniques with modern quilts—both instead of and in addition to regular machine piecing. Appliqué really lends itself to improvisation, which is my favorite method. Plus, I love the versatility of appliqué. It encourages me to use shapes and sizes of fabric that I might shy away from when using traditional piecing methods.

I enjoy cutting my appliqué pieces freehand, which makes each quilt unique. By cutting freehand, I can size the appliqués specifically for the fabrics and style I'm using.

Photo by Beth Vassalo

BETH VASSALO

Seven years ago, Beth Vassalo was inspired to learn how to sew while watching her young daughter create dress-up clothes and accessories with paper and tape. With the help of several books and online sources, Beth learned the basics and was soon regularly sewing, knitting, and crocheting projects for herself and her three daughters.

A few years later, Beth discovered quilting and has been designing and making quilts ever since. She is the co-author of *The Modern Medallion Workbook*, published by Stash Books in spring 2015, and shares her sewing adventures at plumandjune.blogspot.com.

Bowls, 23˝ × 23˝, designed, made, and quilted by Beth Vassalo, 2014

MATERIALS

Unless otherwise noted, all measurements refer to 40˝-wide 100% cotton quilting fabric.

- **Fabric scraps:** total of about 1 yard in a variety of sizes and colors for piecing blocks and for appliqué semicircles (The finished project and instructions feature solids and prints in various shades of purple, green, blue, yellow, white, peach, and gray.)

- **Gray solid:** ½ yard for background

- **Backing:** ⅞ yard

- **Binding:** ⅓ yard

- **Batting:** 31˝ × 31˝

- **Thread:** to coordinate with appliqué fabrics

Cutting

From the purple scraps:

- Cut 2 rectangles 2½″ × 6″ for Blocks 1 and 8.

From the green scraps:

- Cut 1 rectangle 4″ × 6″ for Block 1.

- Cut 1 rectangle 2½″ × 4″ for Block 2.

From the blue scraps:

- Cut 2 rectangles 4″ × 6″ for Blocks 2 and 8.

- Cut 1 rectangle 2″ × 2½″ and 1 rectangle 1″ × 2½″ for Block 2.

- Cut 1 square 4″ × 4″ for Block 4.

- Cut 1 rectangle 5″ × 6″ for Block 6.

From the yellow scraps:

- Cut 1 rectangle 3½″ × 6″ for Block 3.

- Cut 1 rectangle 2½″ × 6″, 1 rectangle 1″ × 4″, and 1 rectangle 2″ × 4″ for Block 4.

- Cut 1 rectangle 1½″ × 6″ for Block 6.

- Cut 1 rectangle 2″ × 4½″ for Block 7.

From the white print scraps:

- Cut 1 rectangle 3″ × 6″, 1 rectangle 2″ × 2½″, and 1 rectangle 1″ × 2½″ for Block 3.

- Cut 1 rectangle 3″ × 6″, 1 rectangle 1½″ × 3½″, and 1 rectangle ¾″ × 3½″ for Block 5.

- Cut 1 rectangle 4½″ × 6″, 1 rectangle 1″ × 2″, and 1 rectangle 1½″ × 2″ for Block 7.

- Cut 1 rectangle 2″ × 6″, 1 rectangle ¾″ × 4½″, and 1 rectangle 1½″ × 4½″ for Block 9.

From the peach scraps:

- Cut 1 rectangle 3½″ × 4¾″ for Block 5.

- Cut 1 rectangle 4¾″ × 4½″ for Block 9.

From the gray background fabric:

- Cut 3 strips 1½″ × width of fabric; subcut into:

  6 rectangles 1½″ × 6″ for block sashing

  3 strips 1½″ × 19″

  1 strip 1½″ × 20″

- Cut 1 strip 3½″ × 20″.

- Cut 1 strip 3½″ × 23″.

Assembling the Block Backgrounds

All seam allowances are ¼". Press after each seam.

 Block 1

Sew the purple 2½" × 6" rectangle to the green 4" × 6" rectangle as shown.

 Block 2

Sew the blue 2" × 2½" and 1" × 2½" rectangles to opposite sides of the green 2½" × 4" rectangle as shown. Sew the 4" × 6" blue rectangle to the top of the pieced unit.

 Block 3

Sew the yellow 3½" × 6" rectangle to the top of the white 3" × 6" rectangle as shown.

 Block 4

Sew the yellow 1" × 4" and 2" × 4" rectangles to 2 opposite sides of the blue 4" × 4" square as shown. Sew the yellow 2½" × 6" rectangle to the top of the pieced section.

 Block 5

Sew the white 1½" × 3½" and ¾" × 3½" rectangles to 2 opposite sides of the peach 3½" × 4¾" rectangle as shown. Sew the remaining white 3" × 6" rectangle to the top of the pieced section.

 Block 6

Sew the blue 4" × 6" rectangle to the left side of the yellow 1½" × 6" rectangle as shown.

 Block 7

Sew the white 1" × 2" and 1½" × 2" rectangles to 2 opposite sides of the yellow 2" × 4½" rectangle as shown. Sew the white 4½" × 6" rectangle to the top of the pieced section.

 Block 8

Sew the blue 4" × 6" rectangle to the top of the purple 2½" × 6" rectangle as shown.

 Block 9

Sew the white ¾" × 4½" and 1½" × 4½" rectangles to 2 opposite sides of the peach 4¾" × 4½" rectangle. Sew the white 2" × 6" rectangle to the top of the pieced section.

Assembling the Quilt

1 Sew 1½″ × 6″ gray sashing strips to the right sides of Blocks 1, 2, 4, 5, 7, and 8.

2 Sew Blocks 1, 2, and 3; 4, 5, and 6; and 7, 8, and 9 together as shown in the quilt assembly diagram.

3 Sew 1½″ × 19″ gray sashing strips to the top and bottom of the center row (Blocks 4/5/6).

4 Sew the top row (Blocks 1/2/3) to the top of the center row. Sew the bottom row (Blocks 7/8/9) to the bottom of the center row.

5 Sew the 1½″ × 19″ gray border strip to the right side of the pieced center.

6 Sew the 1½″ × 20″ gray border strip to the bottom of the pieced center.

7 Sew the 3½″ × 20″ gray border strip to the left side of the pieced center.

8 Sew the 3½″ × 23″ gray border strip to the top of the pieced center.

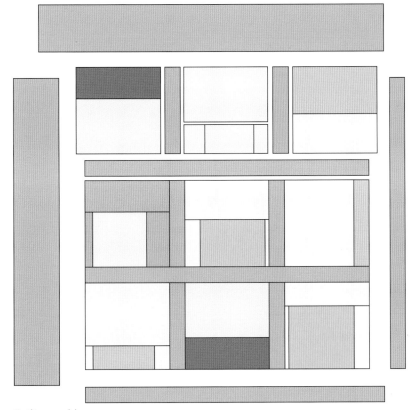

Quilt assembly

TIP Beth chose to quilt the pieced top before adding the appliqués. This is a personal preference, and you may prefer to sew on the appliqués while piecing the blocks or after adding the borders. If you decide to quilt first, keep the appliquéd bowls in mind as you choose a quilting design.

Adding the Appliquéd Bowls

1 To cut the bowl shapes freehand, start by cutting a square or rectangle the length of the straight edge of the semicircle; then cut a semicircle from the piece. 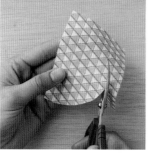 If it helps, mark the curve of the circle on the fabric before you cut. Refer to the list at right for the length of the straight edge.

> **TIP** If you are uncomfortable cutting out the semicircles freehand, draw your own paper pattern freehand or by using a compass.

2 Arrange the bowls on the quilt, placing each within its designated block. To follow Beth's design, see the appliqué placement diagram.

> **TIP** Temporarily place all the semicircles on the quilt before sewing them in place. Stand back and see how you think it looks. Try moving the semicircles around and perhaps even trimming some smaller or to a slightly different shape before sewing them to the quilt.

3 Referring to Basic Machine Appliqué (page 14), machine stitch the bowls to the quilt. Beth chose to straight stitch close to the edge of the perimeter of each semicircle several times.

For block number:	Cut a semicircle (or 2 semicircles) with straight edge(s) no longer than:
Block 1	3½″
Block 2	3″
Block 3	3½″
Block 4	3″ and 1″
Block 5	3½″
Block 6	3″
Block 7	3½″
Block 8	4½″
Block 9	3½″ and 2½″

Appliqué placement

Finishing

1 Refer to Finishing a Quilt (page 150) to layer, baste, and quilt as desired.

2 Refer to Binding (page 151) or use your preferred method to make and attach the binding.

3 If you plan to hang the quilt, refer to Hanging Sleeves (page 154) to add a sleeve.

Beth's Appliqué Tips

For this quilt, I decided to quilt before adding the appliqués for two reasons:

* *I knew I would be using an allover quilting design and I didn't want that design to be on the appliqués, and*

* *I knew I was sewing the appliqués to the quilt using several quilting lines on the edges of the bowls, and I wanted those lines to form a separate part of the quilting.*

My tip for anyone new to appliqué is to try the variety of techniques described in this book and find the method that works best for you. You want to choose a method (or methods) that you enjoy doing as well as the one or more that you most like aesthetically. Learning and practicing these techniques will not only expand your quiltmaking possibilities but will also allow you to at times substitute appliqué for traditional piecing to create a unique look.

Melissa Averinos

Award-winning quilter Melissa Averinos describes her process—whether she is painting or making quilts—as play.

"I feel like I'm always in experiment mode. I love improv, and that's the way I use appliqué and that's the way I piece as well … and that's the way I paint, too. … It's really about the making. … I want to like how the end product looks, but it's more about the experience that I have while I'm making it," she says. This attention to process shows in the spontaneous, joyful style of her appliqué work.

Melissa loves the freedom that raw-edge appliqué gives her to work quickly and improvise as she goes. Working with the materials she has at hand, and often taking inspiration directly from them, she thinks of her appliqué portraits as collages made with fabric as the medium and stitching as the glue. Cutting her fabrics freehand and layering them to create shapes, she enjoys seeing the faces come to life before her eyes, "kind of like a polaroid developing."

Working on a design wall, she tacks her appliqué pieces down with white glue in preparation for stitching them on her longarm machine. Melissa embraces the imperfections that occur as part of this process. She likes to work quickly, throwing fabric up on the wall without worrying about getting it right the first time. Instead, she edits and refines until she is happy with the result, noting that this process prevents her from becoming paralyzed by the desire for or expectation of perfection.

Sharing her work is an important part of Melissa's process. She notes that her series of fabric portraits grew out of a positive response that she received to posting one of her pieces on Instagram.

You can visit Melissa and see more of her work on her website, melissaaverinos.com.

Self Portrait, 51″ × 51″, designed, made, and quilted by Melissa Averinos, 2015

SHARDS
by Casey York

Finished size: 50″ × 70″

THIS PROJECT FEATURES:

- Improv rotary cutting
- Improv arrangement
- Raw-edge appliqué
- Fusible appliqué
- Machine stitching

Improvisational piecing has been popular since the inception of the modern quilting movement, but you don't hear about improvisational appliqué as often. There are many ways to incorporate improv techniques into an appliqué quilt. My method, illustrated by this project, incorporates both improvisational cutting and improvisational arrangement of the appliqués. I find the improvisational process both relaxing and enjoyable, while the use of fusible web makes this a quick and satisfying technique.

Photo by Randall Kahn

CASEY YORK

Casey York is a quilt designer and author known for her bold, minimalist appliqué quilts. For more information about Casey, see About the Author (page 159).

MATERIALS

Unless otherwise noted, all measurements refer to 40˝-wide 100% cotton quilting fabric.

- **White:** 3 yards for pieced background *OR* 1¾ yards if fabric is 90˝+ wide

- **Appliqué fabric:** 1 fat quarter each of 5 different blue solids

- **Backing:** 3½ yards

- **Batting:** 58˝ × 78˝

- **Binding:** ½ yard

- **Double-sided light fusible web:** 15˝ wide, 4 yards

- **Invisible thread:** for machine appliqué, if desired

Cutting

From the white background fabric: Cut or piece a 50˝ × 70˝ panel.

Shards, 50˝ × 70˝, designed, made, and quilted by Casey York, 2014

Preparing the Appliqués

1 Following the manufacturer's instructions, fuse lengths of fusible web to the wrong side of each blue fabric, covering the entire fat quarter.

TIP Covering the entire piece of appliqué fabric with fusible web allows the shapes to be cut improvisationally.

2 Using a rotary cutter and ruler, cut the appliqués. Create triangles by making a series of diagonal cuts along the length of the fabric. You do not need to mark the fabric first, but using a ruler will ensure that the long edges of the appliqués remain straight. Aim to cut 6–10 triangles from each fat quarter.

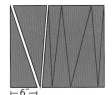

Cut triangles in several shapes and sizes.

3 At this point, all the triangle appliqués are approximately the same length. Use a rotary cutter to trim the wide end of at least half the triangles in each color.

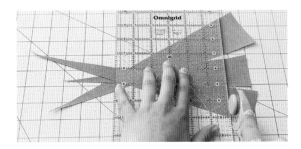

TIP I like to work with appliqués that appear random. You can achieve randomness in the shapes of the triangles by cutting the ends of several at once. Simply lay a group of triangles out with their points facing the same direction. Mix up the pile a little, so the points are pointing in slightly different directions, and then cut through all the wide ends at once.

Assembling the Quilt Top

1 Find the center of the background fabric by folding it in half horizontally and vertically and pressing to form creases. The center will be the point where the creases meet.

2 Begin arranging the appliqués, placing them with the sharp points toward the center of the background, as in the appliqué placement diagram. The appliqués do not need to touch the center point. The diagram provides only a suggested layout; have fun creating your own!

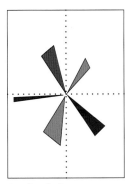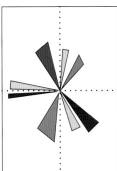

Appliqué placement

TIP To ensure that colors and sizes of appliqués are distributed evenly around the composition, I find it easiest to place the appliqués one color at a time. First, I place two or three appliqués of a single color around the center point, distributing them evenly. Then I place two or three appliqués of another single color between these first appliqués. I repeat for each color until all the colors have been placed. Then I fill in between them as needed.

3 Remove the paper backing from the appliqués as you place them. Do not worry if there are gaps among them, as you will be cutting more appliqués to fill in these gaps in the next steps. When you are satisfied with your arrangement, pin each appliqué in place.

4 Identify any large gaps in the arrangement, making note of their approximate size and shape. Trim the leftover triangle appliqués to fit into these gaps. Remove their backing paper and pin in place.

5 Referring to the fusible manufacturer's directions, use an iron to fuse the appliqués permanently into place. Remove the pins before you press each appliqué. You can press portions of multiple appliqués at once; there is no need to try to press each appliqué individually.

TIP Because the points of the triangles come together in the center of this design, it is easiest to begin pressing from the center and move outward along each appliqué. This allows you to fine-tune the placement of all the individual points to ensure that none overlap.

6 Referring to Basic Machine Appliqué (page 14), use invisible thread and a zigzag or blanket stitch to machine stitch around the edge of each appliqué.

Finishing

1 Refer to Finishing a Quilt (page 150) to layer, baste, and quilt as desired.

2 Refer to Binding (page 151) or use your preferred method to make and attach the binding.

3 If you plan to hang the quilt, refer to Hanging Sleeves (page 154) to add a sleeve.

Casey's Improv Appliqué Tips

The glass shards that inspired this project determined the basic shape and color of the appliqués, but this improvisational technique can be used with many shapes and colors. Although the appliqués are cut with a rotary cutter here, it is also fun to use a pair of scissors to cut out appliqués freehand. When you are freehand cutting, it helps to envision a core shape—a circle, square, crescent, or other shape—to guide your cutting. The goal is to create random appliqué shapes in various sizes that will enable you to design a full and interesting composition.

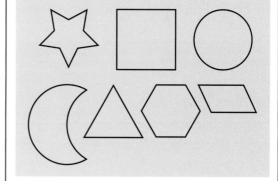

Finishing Your Projects

Although most of the projects in this book are quilts, appliqué is remarkable in that you can adapt it to suit any type (or size) of project you desire. Use these instructions to finish your quilts, or scale down the projects here by using only a few appliqués on a wallhanging or pillow.

Finishing a Quilt

To finish your quilt, cut the backing fabric and batting to measure 4″ larger than the quilt measurements on each side (a total of 8″ larger than the final quilt measurements). Layer the quilt backing, batting, and quilt top, centering the quilt top on the lower layers, and carefully smooth out any wrinkles.

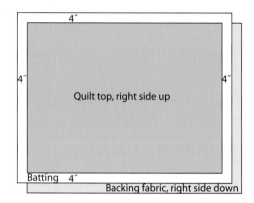

Basting

When the layers are smooth, baste the quilt. There are a number of ways to do this. Traditionally, basting was done by hand using a contrasting thread and a running stitch. Begin in the center of the quilt and baste toward the outer edges, smoothing any wrinkles that form as you stitch. Make your stitches about 1″–2″ long and leave about 1″–2″ between stitches. Using a contrasting colored thread will make the stitches easy to see and remove after quilting.

As an alternative to hand basting, many quilters use pins. When pin basting, place the pins about 4″ apart over the entire surface of the quilt, again starting in the center and moving toward the outer edges. Remove the basting pins as you quilt.

TIP When removing basting pins, leave them open so that they are ready for the next basting project.

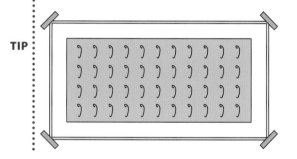

Spray basting is another popular option. In this method, an aerosol adhesive is applied between the layers to "glue" them together for quilting. Wash the quilt after quilting to remove any adhesive residue.

Spray basting is especially well suited to smaller quilted projects. However, because it is only applied between the surfaces of the batting and the backing fabric and quilt top, it does not hold the three layers together as securely as thread basting or pin basting. For this reason, it is a less desirable option for basting quilts twin-size and larger that will be manipulated extensively during the quilting process. If you choose to spray baste your quilt, make sure to follow the manufacturer's directions for the basting spray that you use.

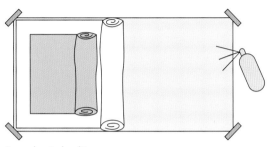

Spray baste backing.

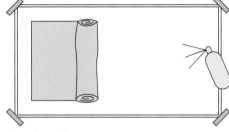

Spray baste batting.

Quilting

Several of the projects in this book include suggestions for quilting; for others, the quilting design is left up to you. In general, I like to quilt around my appliqués, as this emphasizes them. It is not typical for allover quilting designs to cross over from the background fabric onto the appliqués themselves, because this tends to flatten the appliqués and make them fade into the background. However, this is not a rule, and sometimes quilting an allover design across both the background and the appliqués can produce interesting effects. You can also add separate quilted motifs inside the appliqué shapes to embellish them, and I recommend this if the appliqués are particularly large, as it will help keep the layers of the quilt from shifting.

After quilting, trim the batting and backing flush with the quilt top in preparation for binding, and remove any remaining basting pins or threads.

Binding

Just as there are multiple appliqué methods, there are many different ways to make and apply binding to a quilt, and everybody has his or her favorite. I prefer hand-finished double-fold bias binding (page 153); I find that it gives me the smoothest finish and the best mitered corners. Feel free to follow Steps 1–6 (page 152) or use your own favorite method to attach the binding for the projects in this book.

For this method, I cut 2½˝-wide strips of fabric. To calculate how many strips you will need, add 2 × quilt width + 2 × quilt length + 16˝. Divide this sum by 40˝ (the width of fabric). Round up to a whole number to determine how many strips you need to cut. Sew the strips into one continuous strip with diagonal seams. Trim the seam allowance to ¼˝, fold in half lengthwise with wrong sides together, and press.

1 Beginning with the lower edge of your trimmed quilt, pin the binding so that all the raw edges align. Pin until you reach the first corner. Begin stitching at least 12˝ from the end of the binding (the free tail of binding will be necessary when you join the binding strips in Step 4). Using a ¼˝ seam allowance, stitch along the pinned length, stopping ¼˝ before you reach the edge of the quilt.

2 Fold the binding back at a 90° angle as shown and press. Fold the binding back upon itself, parallel to the next edge of the quilt to be sewn; press.

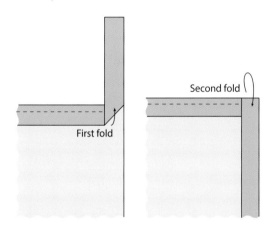

Second fold

First fold

3 Repeat Steps 1 and 2 for the remaining 3 edges of the quilt. When you reach the bottom edge, stop stitching at least 12˝ from the place where you began sewing on the binding.

4 To finish the binding, bring the 2 ends together and overlap them. Trim the ends so that they overlap 2½˝ (or the width of the unfolded binding that you are using). Unfold the binding and align the cut edges at a 90° angle. Stitch on the diagonal, trim, and press the seam.

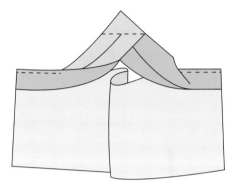

5 Refold the binding and align the raw edges with the raw edges of the quilt; pin in place and stitch.

6 To finish the back, fold the binding around the ¼˝ seam allowance to the back of the quilt. Using a slip stitch or ladder stitch, stitch in place by hand.

MAKING BIAS BINDING

Method 1

1 Square up the fabric. Align your ruler so that the 45° line is parallel to the trued edge; cut along the length of the ruler.

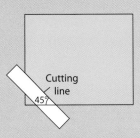

2 Working parallel to the 45° cut you just made, cut strips 2½″ wide (or your preferred width).

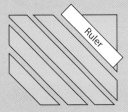

3 Align the ends of the strips as shown in the diagram and stitch together, creating a single long strip of fabric. Trim the dog-ears on the seam allowances. Press the seams open.

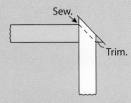

4 Fold the strip in half lengthwise with *wrong* sides together and press.

Method 2

Continuous bias binding involves slicing a square in half diagonally and then sewing the resulting triangles together. You then mark strips, sew again to make a tube, and cut to make a continuous binding strip of the desired length.

1 Cut the fabric for the bias binding so it is a square. For example, if the yardage is ½ yard, cut an 18″ × 18″ square.

2 Cut the square in half diagonally, creating 2 triangles. Using a ¼″ seam allowance, sew the triangles together as shown; press the seam open.

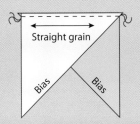

3 Using a ruler, mark the resulting parallelogram with lines spaced the desired width of your binding strips. Cut about 5″ along the first line, as shown.

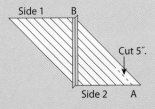

4 Join Side 1 and Side 2 to form a tube. The raw edge at point A will align with the raw edge at point B, allowing the first line to be offset by 1 strip width. With right sides together, pin the raw edges, making sure that the marked lines match up. Sew with a ¼″ seam allowance; press the seam open.

5 Cut along the drawn lines, creating a continuous strip.

6 Fold the entire strip in half lengthwise, *wrong* sides together, and press.

Hanging Sleeves

Many of the quilts in this book are just the right size for being displayed on a wall, and other patterns can be easily adapted to smaller-sized quilts simply by changing the size of the background fabric and the layout of the appliqués. Adding a hanging sleeve on the back allows these projects to be hung from a rod. These instructions are for a 4″-wide sleeve, which is the standard size used for displaying quilts in quilt shows, but you can make the sleeve narrower if the project is smaller and you will only be displaying it in your home.

NOTE: I learned this method from Jacquie Gering; you can learn more about it on her blog, tallgrassprairiestudio.blogspot.com.

1 Measure the width of the quilt at the top. Call this measurement W. Cut or piece a piece of fabric that measures W × 8½″.

2 Hem each 8½″ end of this strip by folding under ¼″ twice and stitching close to the fold.

3 With *wrong* sides together, fold the entire strip in half lengthwise and press to crease. Unfold.

4 Fold each long edge in to meet the center crease and press to crease. Unfold.

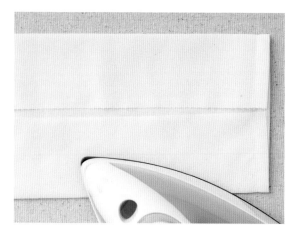

5 With wrong sides together, stitch along the length of the strip using a ¼″ seam. Press the seam open, being careful not to disturb the 2 side creases that you made in Step 4. This seam will be placed against the back of the quilt when you attach the sleeve, so it will not be visible. The opening in the sleeve should form a "D," which allows room for the hanging rod to be inserted without distorting the quilt.

6 Pin the sleeve to the back of the quilt, about ½″ from the top and ½″ in from either edge. Hand stitch along the side creases at the top and bottom, making sure the stitches do not show on the front of the quilt.

Finishing a Pillow

A pillow can be a perfect smaller project to try out a new technique or style. Most of the appliqué patterns in this book are small enough to be made into a pillow. Simply cut the background to the size you wish your finished pillow to be and select the appliqué patterns you wish to use, and you're good to go. To transform your finished appliqué panel into a pillow cover, either follow the instructions below for a simple envelope closure or use your own favorite method.

TIP Pillow forms are available in a range of standard sizes. If you intend to make a pillow, start by selecting the size of the pillow form you'd like to use. Cut the background fabric to this size if you'd like a tightly stuffed pillow, or add 1″ to each dimension for a more loosely stuffed look.

1 If you wish, quilt the front of your pillow cover. If you have embroidered the appliqué piece and you don't wish to quilt it, you will want to protect the back of the stitching. You can do this easily by cutting a piece of lightweight woven fusible interfacing the same size as the appliqué piece and fusing it to the wrong side. The fusible material will hold the fabric in place until you stitch the pillow together, at which point it will be secured inside the side seams.

2 Measure the length and width of your appliquéd pillow front; you will use these dimensions to determine the dimensions of the backing pieces.

3 Determine which way you would like the opening on the pillow back to run—the most common placement is horizontal. For a horizontal opening, divide the length of the pillow in half and then add 3″. Cut 2 pieces the width of the front × this new length.

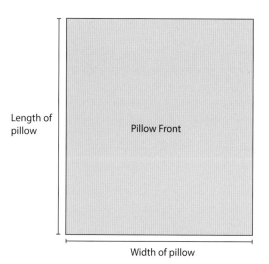

Length of pillow

Pillow Front

Width of pillow

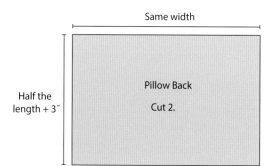

Same width

Half the length + 3″

Pillow Back

Cut 2.

4 Turn a ¼″ fold along a long edge of each of the 2 backing panels and press. Fold another ¼″ and press. Topstitch ⅛″ from each folded edge. These will be the opening edges of the pillow back.

5 Place the pillow front faceup on a flat surface. Place the 2 pillow back panels facedown, aligning the raw edges with those of the pillow front. The finished edges of the panels should overlap at the center of the pillow. Pin in place on all 4 sides.

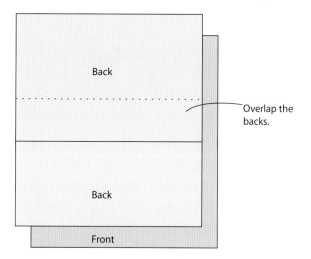

Back

Back

Front

Overlap the backs.

6 Stitch ½″ around the outside edge of the pillow. Press. Trim the corners at a diagonal and turn the pillow inside out.

7 Insert the pillow form.

Resources

The first place to go for information and products is your local quilt shop. If you don't have a shop nearby or desire further information, then try the Internet.

Books

Additional books on appliqué

Mastering Machine Appliqué: The Complete Guide, 2nd Edition, Harriet Hargrave (C&T Publishing, 2002)

Piece by Piece Machine Appliqué, Sharon Schamber and Cristy Fincher (American Quilter's Society, 2007)

Barbara Brackman's Encyclopedia of Appliqué, Barbara Brackman (C&T Publishing, 2009)

The Ultimate Appliqué Guidebook, Annie Smith (C&T Publishing, 2010)

Scrappy Bits Appliqué, Shannon Brinkley (Stash Books, 2014)

The Modern Appliqué Workbook, Jenifer Dick (Stash Books, 2014)

Alison Glass Appliqué, Alison Glass (Lucky Spool Media, 2014)

The Quilter's Appliqué Workshop, Kevin Kosbab (Interweave, 2014)

Modern Appliqué Illusions, Casey York (Stash Books, 2014)

About Face, Shruti Dandekar (self-published, 2014)

Books that feature appliqué techniques

Inspired to Sew by Bari J., Bari J. Ackerman (Stash Books, 2011)

Quilting from Little Things, Sarah Fielke (Krause Publishing, 2011)

Denyse Schmidt: Modern Quilts, Traditional Inspiration, Denyse Schmidt (Stewart, Tabori & Chang, 2012)

Hand Quilted with Love, Sarah Fielke (CICO Books, 2013)

Savor Each Stitch, Carolyn Friedlander (Lucky Spool Media, 2014)

Present Perfect: 25 Gifts to Sew & Bestow, Betz White (Interweave, 2014)

Materials

Batting

The Warm Company
warmcompany.com
Warm & White Needled Cotton Batting

Fusible web

Pellon
pellonprojects.com
805 Wonder-Under

Glue

Elmer's
elmers.com
Disappearing Purple School Glue Sticks, Washable White School Glue

Roxanne
colonialneedle.com
Glue-Baste-It

Mini iron; bias tape makers

Clover
clover-usa.com
Mini Iron, Bias Tape Makers

Nonstick appliqué pressing sheets

Bear Thread Designs, Inc.
bearthreaddesigns.com
Appliqué Pressing Sheet

C&T Publishing
ctpub.com
Silicone Release Paper

Embroidery hoops

Darice, Inc.
darice.com
Spring Tension Embroidery Hoop

Thread

Aurifil
aurifil.com
50-weight Cotton Thread and Invisible Nylon Thread

Superior Threads
superiorthreads.com
Clear MonoPoly Thread

Wash-away appliqué paper

C&T Publishing
ctpub.com
Wash-Away Appliqué Sheets